WHERE ARE POOR HOUSEHOLDS?

The Spatial Distribution of Poverty and
Deprivation in Ireland

Brian Nolan
Christopher T. Whelan
James Williams

Oak Tree Press

Dublin
in association with
Combat Poverty Agency

Oak Tree Press
Merrion Building
Lower Merrion Street
Dublin 2, Ireland

A catalogue record of this book is
available from the British Library.

ISBN 1-86076-085-6

This study forms part of the Combat Poverty Agency's Research
Series, in which it is No. 25. The views expressed in this report
are the authors' own and not necessarily those of the
Combat Poverty Agency.

Printed in Ireland by Colour Books Ltd.

Contents

List of Tables

List of Maps

Acknowledgements

This study arises from a major research programme being carried out at the Economic and Social Research Institute and sponsored by the Department of Social, Community and Family Affairs and the Combat Poverty Agency. It draws on a new and unique data source, the 1994 Living in Ireland Survey, which constitutes the Irish element of the European Community Household Panel initiated by Eurostat the Statistical Office of the European Communities. The Combat Poverty Agency has provided specific funding for this project and we would like to express our appreciation of their support.

In carrying out this study we have benefited enormously from the detailed comment on earlier drafts by Helen Johnston of the Combat Poverty Agency and from suggestions provided by the Department of Social, Community and Family Affairs and two anonymous referees. Jim Walsh of the Combat Poverty Agency and our Economic and Social Research Institute colleagues Tony Fahey and Dorothy Watson have been generous in allowing us to take advantage of their experience in this area. The final version of this study has gained from the opportunity we had to present and discuss our results at an Economic and Social Research Institute seminar and also at a special Geographical Society of Ireland conference on *Poor People, Poor Places* held in the National University of Ireland, Maynooth in September 1996.

We also gratefully acknowledge the assistance of Joan O'Flynn of the Combat Poverty Agency and Phil Browne, Pat Hopkins and Maura Rohan of the Economic and Social Research Institute. The staff of the ESRI's survey unit, the interviewers and the survey respondents are all thanked for their special efforts, without which this study would not have been possible.

The authors accept full responsibility for the content and for any errors and omissions.

Brian Nolan
Christopher T. Whelan
James Williams

Foreword

Introduction

The aim of the Combat Poverty Agency is to work for the prevention
and decrease of poverty and social exclusion and the reduction of in-
equality in Ireland by striving for change which will promote a fairer
and more just, equitable and inclusive society. Particularly relevant
in this context is its objective to address the causes and consequences
of poverty by tackling the problems that are manifested in disadvantaged urban and rural communities.

It is known that particular communities suffer from cumulative
disadvantage, and that in some cases these communities are spatially
concentrated. As documented in the National Anti-Poverty Strategy[1]
a number of types of area have been identified as being at particular
risk of disadvantage. These include decaying inner city areas, large
public housing estates on city and town peripheries, and isolated and
underdeveloped rural areas.

However, questions arise relating to the geography of poverty and
disadvantage. Key questions include:

- Is poverty concentrated in particular areas?

- If poverty is concentrated in particular areas what is the extent of
  that concentration?

- Where are the concentrations of poverty?

- Why are there concentrations of poverty?

- What are the characteristics of such concentrations of poverty?

- What can be done about reducing concentrations of poverty?

These questions have prompted the Combat Poverty Agency to undertake a programme of research which attempts to address some of

---

[1] The National Anti-Poverty Strategy (NAPS), *Sharing in Progress*, was published in April 1997 and is available from the NAPS Unit in the Department
of Social, Community and Family Affairs.

these issues. This report examines some of the spatial aspects of poverty and deprivation in Ireland.

Background to the Research

The Combat Poverty Agency commissioned Brian Nolan, Chris Whelan and James Williams to undertake a study on the spatial aspects of poverty and deprivation utilising 1987 and 1994 national household survey data and 1986 and 1991 Census of Population data. This study builds on earlier (unpublished) work undertaken by James Williams for the Agency in 1993 on *Spatial Variations in Deprivation Surrogates — A Preliminary Analysis* which was based mainly on small area population statistics from the 1986 Census of Population.

The spatial distribution of poverty and its implications have recently been the subject of discussion and debate at theoretical, policy and practice levels in Ireland and Europe. In particular, discussions on the problems of concentrations of poverty (sometimes referred to as poverty "black spots") and on whether an urban "underclass" is emerging have been topical.

One of the areas which is of particular interest is the concept of cumulative disadvantage. People experiencing cumulative disadvantage are often referred to as living in poverty "black spots", where it has been suggested that the experience of being poor and living in such an area is a qualitatively different, and usually worse experience than being poor and living in a non-disadvantaged area.

A number of researchers are working in this area in Ireland and in 1996 the Geographical Society of Ireland held a conference on *Poor People, Poor Places*. This conference brought together the main researchers and practitioners in this field to discuss issues relating to the analysis of the spatial aspects of poverty in Ireland.[2] Work on the geography of poverty has also been undertaken in Northern Ireland, the United Kingdom and in Europe. A number of key issues which have been emerging from this work relate to:

• Data availability on poverty and appropriate scale levels;

• The appropriate unit of analysis/level of data disaggregation;

• The feasibility of constructing deprivation measures and indices;

---

[2] Conference papers are being prepared for publication.

- Use to which the information is put (descriptive, analytical, targeting, interventions);

- Implications for national, regional and local policy.

The aim of this study is to examine what types of areas have particularly high rates of poverty, the extent to which people living in poverty or who are disadvantaged are concentrated in particular areas and whether such patterns have changed over time.

As a starting point data on the concentration of poor households in specific areas or types of area are vital in teasing out the role of area effects among the causal processes producing and reproducing poverty. It is also important in assessing the scope for targeting resources (such as public services) spatially in order to maximise the number of poor households reached.

Methodological Issues

Ways of measuring geographical concentrations of poverty and deprivation have been the subject of debate. The main thrust of many of the concerns relate to: (i) whether it is possible to identify dimensions of deprivation using Census data which does not contain any information on income or levels of deprivation; and (ii) the choice of area base.

The issue of constructing an overall index of socio-structural disadvantage is dealt with in Chapter 9, section 9.4 of the study. This methodological debate is critical in terms of identifying appropriate responses to the varied socio-demographic processes which can lead to distinctly different outcomes. Further work on the methodology of identifying poverty and disadvantage at a spatial level and understanding the processes which result in concentrations of poverty will be important.

The choice of area base is also important. Should poverty and deprivation be analysed at an individual, household, community or area level? What difference does it make? Often this depends on the data available and our understanding of poverty. Information on household poverty is available from national household surveys; however it is not possible to analyse poverty at a local level using national household surveys. The Census of Population allows measurement at a more local level, but information is not available for households or on poverty. Therefore proxies have to be used. These are fairly well developed now — but debate hinges around the level of disaggregation/aggregation of the data. For example, some analysis at the Dublin level shows Dublin to have around average levels of disadvantage.

However, it is known that Dublin contains some of the richest areas in the country and also some of the poorest — this heterogeneity can be masked by county and county borough level analysis where the two extremes can balance each other out. This report gives a broad national picture of where large spatial concentrations of poverty exist. However, national studies need to be complemented by local studies which, at the local level, can elucidate processes of deprivation and adaptation and thus facilitate the formulation of local policy responses.

Key Findings

Some of the key findings of the report are summarised here, in point form, to set the policy implications of the report in context. Details of the findings make up the main content of the report.

1. Poverty is not, to any significant degree, concentrated in any particular type of area.
2. The highest risk of poverty was observed for villages and towns with populations of less than three thousand.
3. Between 1986 and 1994 the risk of poverty fell for households located in open country, but rose for households in Dublin city and county.
4. While the proportion of poor households located in Dublin increased significantly between 1987 and 1994, the number of poor households found there is still only as high as its share of households in the overall population.
5. Housing tenure is a more significant factor in explaining the distribution of poverty risks and the concentration of poverty than location *per se.*
6. High risks of poverty are associated with being a local authority tenant and the level of risk for such households increased significantly between 1987 and 1994.
7. Local authority tenant–purchasers, although less disadvantaged than local authority renters also had a high poverty risk, which increased between 1987 and 1994.
8. However, because the overall numbers in local authority housing have fallen households in public sector housing did not make up a greater proportion of poor households in 1994.

9.   Households in local authority housing made up about 50% of those living in poverty, in both 1987 and 1994. It is therefore apparent that one in two poor households are located outside public sector housing.

10. In Dublin, almost 70% of households renting local authority housing are living in poverty.

11. By 1994, 20% of poor households were located in local authority housing in Dublin city and county.

12. The disadvantage experienced by local authority households in general, and their worsening over the 1987–1994 period, was found to be mainly attributable to the social and demographic characteristics of the households involved. These characteristics of the head of household included: social class, education, labour force status, proportion of time unemployed, lone parenthood and number of children in the household.

13. However, the social and demographic characteristics of households do not fully explain the relatively high poverty rates of local authority renters or their relative deterioration over time. In rural areas, socio-demographic characteristics account for most of the disparities between different tenure types. In urban areas however, particularly in Dublin, the odds of local authority renters being poor remains more than six times greater than that for owner occupiers, suggesting a relationship between poverty and local authority renting in urban areas.

14. Using 1991 census data the 30% of DEDs[3] with the highest rates of unemployment contain 58% of the unemployed and 39% of the population aged 15 and over. Therefore, to reach a majority of the unemployed an area which also contained about 40% of the adult population would have to be covered. In addition, the areas are not spatially contiguous and may be widely distributed across the country.

15. In Dublin (city and county) the 30% of wards with the highest unemployment rates were found to contain 53% of the unemployed and 28% of the adult population.

---

[3] DED = District Electoral Division, which is the most disaggregated unit of analysis available from the Small Area Population Statistics derived from the Census of Population. There are a total of 3,400 DEDs throughout the country. There are 322 DEDs (referred to as electoral wards) in Dublin city and Dublin county.

16. The 30% of DEDs with the highest percentage of their population in the unskilled manual social group contained 46% of unskilled manual persons compared with 28% of all persons.

17. In Dublin the 30% of wards with the highest percentage in the unskilled manual class contained 55% of unskilled manual persons and 27% of all persons.

18. The 20% of DEDs with the highest proportion of their households renting from the local authority contained a total of 82% of all local authority rented households compared to 37% of all households.

19. At a national level, Dublin contains a substantial over-concentration of local authority rentals — approximately 75% more than would be expected if local authority rentals were distributed on a pro rata basis with all households.

20. In Dublin the 20% of wards with the highest proportions of local authority renters contained 67% of all local authority rentals in Dublin compared to only 19% of all households, and thus had 3.5 times as many local authority rentals as would be found if they were distributed on a pro rata basis with all households. Dublin contains a substantial concentration of local authority renters in some areas.

Policy Implications of the Findings

National Policy

The most significant development in tackling poverty at a national level has been the National Anti-Poverty Strategy (NAPS) which was launched in April 1997. This strategy has been endorsed in *Partnership 2000*, the national agreement between the government and social partners. The NAPS is a major initiative to tackle poverty and social exclusion in Ireland by targeting five key themes for coordinated action by all government departments and state agencies at national, regional and local level. These are:

• Educational disadvantage

• Unemployment, particularly long-term unemployment

• Income adequacy

• Disadvantaged urban areas

• Rural poverty.

Essentially the NAPS recognises that in addressing poverty it is necessary to identify and tackle the causes of poverty. In this context it is important to examine the operation of the labour market: unemployment and especially long-term unemployment has been shown to be a fundamental cause of poverty. It has also been found that the experience of unemployment is very unequally shared. The education system, in the absence of counter measures, can reproduce inequalities and poverty. However, the education system has a key role to play in providing a route out of poverty. The tax and social welfare systems are also critical in addressing poverty. Thus, national policy actions are required to meet the targets set in each of these theme areas to address the key causes of poverty.

The NAPS also recognises the spatial dimension of poverty. The strategy document acknowledges at the outset, however, that disadvantage and unemployment affect virtually every area in Ireland and that people living in poverty or who are unemployed are not singularly clustered in major urban centres. Nevertheless, the Strategy does recognise that particular communities do suffer from cumulative disadvantage and for such people, it is likely that the cumulative effect is to intensify their experience of disadvantage. This recognition is followed through into the key action areas where the tackling of poverty in disadvantaged urban areas and addressing rural poverty are identified as two main concerns.

The approach adopted by the National Anti-Poverty Strategy is very much supported by the findings of this report on the spatial aspects of poverty and deprivation. The report states in its conclusions:

> "Area-based strategies cannot be a panacea for spatially pervasive problems of poverty and unemployment. National economic and social policies are vital. Confronted by the evidence that poverty and unemployment are not concentrated in a limited set of areas the conclusion that the principle objective of area-based interventions should relate to improving the design and implementation of national policy seems to be a compelling one. However, our capacity to distinguish between poor and non-poor households on the basis of tenure suggests that there may still be an important case to be made for targeting-related arguments."

Thus the report argues that the approach to tackling poverty should be driven at the national level. This is at the very core of the NAPS and one supported by the Agency. However, it does recognise that area-based strategies have a role to play.

Area-Based Strategies

The NAPS recognises that there is a need to examine the consequences of high levels and concentrations of poverty which can lead to a threat to the social fabric of the country and incur high economic costs. In addition, there is thought to be a complex relationship where the consequences of poverty can become causes: a cyclical effect which can lead to the reproduction of poverty, and/or the deepening of intergenerational poverty in some areas and communities. The NAPS sets out targets and policy actions to be achieved in addressing disadvantage in urban areas and rural poverty.

A wide range of spatial interventions have been a popular approach to addressing poverty in Ireland in the late 1980s and 1990s. A number of reasons have been identified for this:[4]

• Retrenchment in public expenditure in the 1980s heightened the need for greater selectivity and targeting of resources in addressing economic and social problems;

• A spatial dimension to the growing polarisation between the rich and poor was becoming more apparent, especially in some urban areas; and

• A new localism was emerging in public policy, at both EU and national level.

Within the broad range of spatial anti-poverty initiatives, three discrete applications of the geographical dimension have been identified:

(i)   Targeting of resources (positive spatial discrimination)

(ii)   Co-ordination of services (local planning)

(iii) Economic and social regeneration (local development).

The findings of this report relate mainly to the first dimension and brings into question the extent to which resources can be targeted if poverty is not spatially concentrated. As highlighted in the findings presented above even though households living in local authority housing make up about half of those living in poverty, one in two poor households are located outside local authority housing. A study on educational disadvantage found that approximately 16% of the school

---

[4] See Walsh, J (1996) *Tackling Poverty Through Spatial Interventions*. Paper delivered at the Annual Conference of the Geographical Society of Ireland: Poor People, Poor Places. Available from the Combat Poverty Agency.

going population were educationally disadvantaged.[5] While the concentration of disadvantage across the country was greatest in Dublin,
in absolute numbers the greatest percentage of disadvantaged stu-
dents (61%) were found in rural areas, followed by Dublin (at 25%).
The study also found, however, that the main scheme at that time
which was targeted at pupils from disadvantaged backgrounds at
primary level, (the Scheme of Assistance to Schools in Designated
Areas of Disadvantage) reached only 30% of disadvantaged pupils.
It therefore appears that while the identification of geographical concentrations of disadvantage can assist in selecting areas for targeting
resources the extent to which this approach can be used to reduce
poverty is limited.

Nevertheless, as discussed in this report on spatial aspects of poverty and deprivation there are other valid reasons for area-based approaches to tackling poverty and disadvantage. These include improving the co-ordination of services at a local level, and the promotion of local economic and social regeneration and empowering local
people through greater participative structures. A number of evaluations of area-based programmes, in both urban and rural areas, suggest that there have been significant benefits in adopting an area-
based approach to tackling poverty for these reasons. Thus, a spatial
dimension is important and further work in this area which can better inform the most appropriate scale for spatial interventions would
be extremely useful.

Role of Local Government

The recent White Paper on the reform of local government[6] envisages
a future partnership between local authorities and community groups
to meet the challenges of poverty and social exclusion. It is proposed
that an integrated local government and local development system
will come into place in the year 2000. The White Paper believes that
a renewed system of local government can provide a clearer focus for
the effective delivery of a wider range of public services, for the better
development and well-being of local communities, and for promoting
local development and enterprise.

---

[5] See Kellaghan, Weir, Ó hUallacháin and Morgan (1995) *Educational Disadvantage in Ireland*. Department of Education, Combat Poverty Agency and
the Educational Research Centre.
[6] Department of the Environment (1996) *Better Local Government: A Programme for Change*. Dublin: Stationery Office.

From a spatial dimension of addressing poverty some opportunities in the reform of local government have been identified.[7] The opportunities include:

- A more co-ordinated, integrated, coherent and better understood approach to local development;

- A better structure for mainstreaming local responses; and

- The increased involvement of local authorities, along with partnerships and community groups in tackling poverty and social exclusion at the local level.

A number of threats have also been identified. These include:

- The possibility that local authorities will subordinate and restrict the role of local partnerships; and

- The possibility that local authorities will be unable to target resources towards those most in need and therefore will be unable to tackle social exclusion effectively.

The National Anti-Poverty Strategy envisages a key role for local government in tackling urban and rural disadvantage. In particular, in tackling urban disadvantage NAPS is committed to developing further appropriate indicators of poverty and disadvantage and using this information to monitor changes at a local level. This study can contribute directly to the development of that work.

In addressing rural disadvantage it is envisaged that a renewed system of local government will provide a more effective delivery to a range of public services. Information on the levels of disadvantage and exclusion in rural areas will be important in this regard. This issue is discussed further below.

Information on the spatial aspects of poverty and deprivation will therefore be important in informing local authorities about levels of disadvantage in their areas and should provide a base on which they can develop local anti-poverty strategies. One area where this will be vitally important will be in the provision of social housing.

---

[7] See paper for the Community Directors Forum, 23 May 1997 on *The Implications of the Proposed Reform of Local Government*.

Housing Policy

The authors of this study claim that housing tenure is a more important factor in explaining the distribution of poverty risks and the concentration of poverty than location *per se*. There are high risks of poverty associated with being a local authority tenant and the level of risk for such households increased significantly between 1987 and 1994. The authors attribute this worsening risk, at least in part, to the operation of housing policy over the period. This period has seen a decline in the building programme and high sales of local authority housing which has sharply depleted local authority housing stock. The evidence of an increased risk of poverty for local authority tenants between 1987 and 1994 is consistent with a process of residualisation.

There has been a deterioration in the quality of life in public housing as evidenced by a number of factors:

- Increased polarisation between public and private tenures, with public housing overwhelmingly catering for unemployed people and other disadvantaged groups;

- The emergence of spatial concentrations of poverty associated with public housing;

- Worsening physical environment in both new-build suburban sites and inner city flats;

- Ineffective and inefficient housing management systems;

- Growing problems of crime, vandalism, joy riding and drug abuse;

- Increased alienation and disaffection among residents in public housing areas; and

- Unmet social needs among children, elderly, lone parents and people with disabilities.

It has also been observed that while the deterioration in the social standing of public housing has been general throughout the sector, it has affected urban and rural areas differently. In general, while the problems of poverty and unemployment may be just as great in rural as in urban public housing, in rural areas it is more dispersed and has generally avoided the concentration of deprived households in large single-class estates. In contrast, in urban areas there are large concentrations of public housing, often poorly serviced and segregated from better-off housing areas. This has led, in some cases, to high concentrations of social problems in urban social housing. This raises the question noted earlier — is the experience of being poor and living in such an area qualitatively different and worse than being poor and living in a non-disadvantaged area?

This finding of this study raises a number of issues in this area.

(1) Research

- The need for further work to examine the quality of life on disadvantaged local authority housing estates;[8]

- The need to explore further the extent of poverty and disadvantage in public housing estates in rural areas and in particular estates on the fringes of small towns and villages.

(2) Policy

The need to address the role of social housing at national policy and local delivery level. While there are a number of initiatives currently in place to address many of the problems of the social housing sector it has been argued that they do not go far enough.[9]
For example:

- Initiatives in support of social housing co-exist with a continuing strong emphasis in overall housing policy on home ownership. These initiatives do not provide an effective counter balance to the residualising and marginalising effect on the social housing sector which arises from the intensive promotion of home ownership as the normal housing tenure;

- Developments such as tenant participation and estate-based management have been slow to percolate through the local authorities;

- Remedial works on run-down estates have had an inadequate community development dimension;

- Housing initiatives have been poorly integrated with each other and with local level activities and agencies such as the health boards, education and training services, local employment opportunities etc; and

---

[8] The Combat Poverty Agency, with the Howard Foundation are undertaking a research project on living conditions in public housing estates, in Dublin, other major cities and provincial towns.
[9] See Fahy and Watson (1995) *An Analysis of Social Housing Need*. Dublin: ESRI for a discussion of some of these issues.

- The resources available have not been sufficient to match the needs in these areas.

This report on the spatial distribution of poverty has identified concentrations of poverty and disadvantage in public housing estates especially in urban areas. There is therefore an urgent need to tackle this issue.

Rural Issues

The findings of this study show that between 1987 and 1994 the risk of poverty fell for households located in open country. This is consistent with the recent report on national levels of poverty[10] which found a substantial decline in the risk of poverty for farm households over this period. This was largely because 1986, the year covered by the 1987 survey was a particularly bad one for farming and farm incomes have improved substantially since then. Nevertheless, there is evidence which clearly suggests that there is a group of small farmers, many of them elderly, with a low level of educational attainment and a relatively high proportion of direct payments as a proportion of their income who are living in or at risk of poverty.

One of the main characteristics of poverty in rural Ireland is its seemingly invisible nature. It is important in identifying poverty in rural areas that the people who are poor or who are at greatest risk of poverty are identified, ie. the heterogeneity of rural areas needs to be recognised. Rural areas, unlike some urban areas, do not present homogeneous areas of advantage and disadvantage. Rural areas are more diverse and the experience is often individual and dispersed over a greater geographic area. However, it is important to note that there are also concentrations of poverty in predominantly rural areas. Other research[11] has noted that concentrations of poverty exist in public housing estates on the fringes of small towns and villages. This report on the spatial aspects of poverty has found high risks of poverty associated with living in small towns and villages.

---

[10] See Callan, Nolan, Whelan, B.J. Whelan, C.T. and Williams (1996) *Poverty in the 1990s: Evidence from the Living in Ireland Survey*. Dublin: Oak Tree Press, in association with the ESRI and Combat Poverty Agency.
[11] See Curtin, Haase and Tovey (1996) *Poverty in Rural Ireland: A Political Economy Perspective*. Dublin: Oak Tree Press in association with the Combat Poverty Agency.

A study on educational disadvantage, referred to earlier[12], found that about 60% of pupils defined as educationally disadvantaged live in rural areas. The study concluded that the criteria for identification of disadvantaged pupils in rural areas needed to differ in some key respects from the criteria used to identify disadvantage in urban areas. Revised criteria are now being used. The study also suggested that the nature of interventions also require to be different and more focused on individuals and sharing of resources, rather than solely school-based or area-based interventions.

These conclusions are relevant to this study. It is clear from this report that it would be useful to examine the risk and distribution of rural poverty in more detail. This will require the development of indicators appropriate to the identification of poverty in rural areas and exploration of effective interventions to address it. In this context, the implementation of policies at a national level may be more effective than area-based interventions. However, there are undoubtedly worthwhile initiatives which can be undertaken at local level. This requires identifying social groups at local level who are experiencing poverty and disadvantage rather than identifying "poor areas" *per se*.

Future Issues

The publication of this report on the spatial aspects of poverty and disadvantage is part of an ongoing research programme. Other issues which will be further explored in future are: the concept of cumulative disadvantage; the links between housing tenure and poverty; and the nature of rural poverty.

Work is currently ongoing on a project exploring the manner in which deprivation and poverty becomes concentrated among certain groups and types of households. In particular, it will look at the ways in which cumulative disadvantage arises from a combination of class background, educational failure, labour market marginalisation and marital and parental status, and seek to identify the important processes contributing to cumulative disadvantage and the extent to which these may have changed in recent years.

---

[12] Kellaghan, Weir, Ó hUallacháin and Morgan (1995) *Educational Disadvantage in Ireland*. Department of Education, Combat Poverty Agency and the Educational Research Centre.

On housing, the Agency and the Howard Foundation are undertaking a study on the quality of life in public housing estates. It is intended that the study, which will take a case study approach, will bring important new insights to bear on existing knowledge about public housing by generalising localised data on living conditions and on the impact of various policy initiatives. The research will enable connections to be made between the local experience and the national picture.

As highlighted above further work is required on identifying indicators appropriate for examining the nature of poverty in rural areas so that effective strategies for tackling rural poverty can be designed and implemented.

Concluding Remarks

The Agency believes this study can make an important contribution to our understanding of the spatial dimensions of poverty and disadvantage, which is particularly timely with regard to the implementation of the National Anti-Poverty Strategy, our current national emphasis on area-based strategies and the reform of local government. The Agency acknowledges the work of Brian Nolan, Chris Whelan and James Williams in producing this report which clearly presents a geographical picture of the distribution and risk of poverty throughout Ireland. In addition the report searches for reasons to explain these patterns — work which is currently ongoing.

In the production of this report various people read and commented in detail on earlier drafts. We would like to thank them for their insights and contributions. The Agency also welcomed the input of the Department of Social, Community and Family Affairs/ESRI/Combat Poverty Agency Survey Management Committee who managed this project.

Combat Poverty Agency

May, 1998

Executive Summary

Key Questions

To what extent is poverty in Ireland concentrated in particular areas or types of area, what causal processes underlie the spatial distribution of poverty, and what are the implications for policy? These are the questions addressed by this study. The answers are particularly important in helping to clarify the rationale for area-based strategies and their role in an overall anti-poverty strategy.

The arguments advanced for area-based interventions often take, as a starting point, the notion that unemployment, low income and deprivation are concentrated in certain communities and areas. Devoting resources to such areas can then be justified on the basis that it is an effective way of targeting the poor, that such areas face particular obstacles which need to be addressed, or that being poor in such an area is qualitatively different and worse than being poor elsewhere. However, the fact that some communities and areas have very high poverty rates does not necessarily mean that a high proportion of the poor live in those areas. Special treatment and prioritisation for such highly disadvantaged areas can be justified even if they contain only a minority of the poor, but designing the appropriate policies requires a clear understanding of the processes at work, what makes these areas different and what the policies are intended to achieve.

Data Sources

The data employed in the study come from the large-scale household surveys carried out by the Economic and Social Research Institute in 1987 and 1994, and from the 1986 and 1991 Census of Population Small Area Statistics. With the household survey data, poverty is measured using both relative income poverty lines and a combination of relative income lines and non-monetary indicators of deprivation. No income information is obtained in the Census of Population, but it does allow analysis of the spatial distribution of unemployment, social classes and tenure types, all of which are related to poverty and disadvantage.

Spatial Concentration of Poverty

On the basis of the household surveys it is clear that poverty is not concentrated in any particular type of area, whether it be rural areas, villages, small or large towns or cities. The overall risk of poverty is not especially high in the cities, or in Dublin in particular — if anything it is lower than in villages and very small towns. Between 1987 and 1994 the risk of being poor fell for households located in purely rural areas, but rose for those located in Dublin. Even so, the poor are not over-concentrated in Dublin, in the sense that Dublin has about the same share of poor households as it has of all households.

The Impact of Housing Tenure

Housing tenure is in fact a better predictor of poverty risk than the type of area in which the household is located. Local authority tenants have a relatively high risk of being in poverty: in 1994 over half such households were on relatively low income and experiencing basic forms of deprivation, the most stringent of the poverty criteria employed in the study. Between 1987 and 1994 the risk of poverty had increased for local authority tenants, as had the gap between them and households owning their own house.

The greatest increase in poverty risk for local authority renters between 1987 and 1994, and the widest gap between them and owner-occupiers in 1994, was in Dublin. By 1994, seven out of ten households renting local authority housing in Dublin were on low income and experiencing basic deprivation. Local authority tenant-purchasers, although significantly less disadvantaged, still had above average risks of poverty and saw a significant deterioration in their situation between 1987 and 1994. This still meant that in 1994 only about one in five poor households was in local authority housing (rented or in a tenant-purchase scheme) in Dublin. So a relatively very high risk for certain households still translates into a less than dramatic degree of concentration of poor households in these terms.

The relatively high risk of poverty facing local authority tenants can be mostly but not entirely understood by reference to the social class composition, education, labour force status and experience and demographic profile of the households concerned. These socio-demographic characteristics of households are also seen to account for most of the change in the pattern of poverty rates across area and tenure types between 1987 and 1994. However, households renting local authority housing in urban areas have a higher probability of being poor than these characteristics alone would suggest, and this has become more pronounced between 1987 and 1994. This could arise for a number of reasons. The first is that there are other characteristics of the household and its members which influence the risk of being in poverty, which are disproportionately found among those in urban local authority rented housing, and which have not been included in our analysis. A second is that being in urban local authority rented housing itself increases the risk of being in poverty compared with living elsewhere for otherwise similar households.

Finally, it could be that the causal relationship works the other way: it is not so much that those in urban local authority rented housing are more likely to be poor than other similar households, but that the poor are more likely to be selected into local authority housing or that the non-poor are selected out. All three factors could of course be at work together, but it will be a priority in future research to try to assess their respective contributions to the excess risk of these households.

Evidence from the Census

Moving on from the household survey data, analysis of the Census Small Area Statistics for 1991 produced results that were consistent with the findings from the household surveys. The Census data show that unemployment rates vary somewhat across the counties but a great deal more across the much smaller District Electoral Divisions (DEDs) within counties. Certain DEDs have extremely high unemployment rates, in some cases higher than one-third of the labour force. However, the degree of concentration of unemployment this implies is again limited. For example, Dublin city and county contain one-third of the unemployed, compared with 30 per cent of the adult population.

Even when one groups together the one-tenth of DEDs with the highest unemployment rates — which are not of course located beside one another — these are seen to contain 30 per cent of the unemployed and 15 per cent of the adult population. To reach a majority of the unemployed, one would have to target DEDs containing about 40

per cent of the adult population. Looking at the smaller unit of electoral wards within Dublin, to reach half the unemployed in Dublin
one would have to target wards containing about 30 per cent of the
adult population.

The spatial distribution in the Census of those in the unskilled
manual social class is rather similar in terms of degree of concentration. The distribution of households renting from local authorities is
however more heavily concentrated, particularly in and within Dublin. About 43 per cent of households renting from local authorities are
located in Dublin, and over 80 per cent of these are contained in
fewer than one-third of Dublin's electoral wards.

Elsewhere the small area Census data relating to unemployment,
social class, tenure and distribution of farms by size has been used to
create a composite overall measure of "deprivation". This route is not
pursued in the present study because, given that these variables are
not measures of deprivation but rather determinants of deprivation,
whose relative ability to predict poverty at this level of aggregation is
an unknown, there is no satisfactory way of deciding independently
on the weights to be attributed to each of the variables.

Implications for Policy

The finding that poverty and unemployment are spatially pervasive,
not concentrated in a small number of areas, means that they can
only be effectively tackled through policies designed and implemented at national level. Area-based policies encompassing much or
all of the country may of course play a part in such a strategy, particularly as a means of enhancing local participation and co-
ordination of effort. In addition, policies devoting resources to specific
highly disadvantaged communities and thus explicitly not expected to
reach a majority of poor people can have an important role if they
focus on identifying and overcoming the particular obstacles facing
people living in those areas in their efforts to escape poverty. The results of this study suggest that both housing policy and the gamut of
policies directed towards those living in local authority rented housing should receive priority.

Chapter 1

Introduction

This study analyses the spatial distribution of poverty in Ireland over time, employing the new data from the 1994 Living in Ireland Survey together with the ESRI 1987 Survey of Living Conditions, and the Census of Population Small Area Statistics for 1986 and 1991. Area-based strategies have become a central part of public policy aimed at combating poverty, but the underlying assumptions concerning the manner in which household and spatial factors combine to create patterns of cumulative disadvantage need to be brought out and carefully examined in the light of the evidence. This report is intended to contribute to such a process.

A detailed comparison of the overall extent of poverty in the 1994 and 1987 household surveys is provided in Callan et al., (1996): here we go beyond that study to focus on the spatial perspective. We first outline in Chapter 2 the range of arguments advanced for area-based interventions, to provide the context in which the study is being carried out. Chapter 3 describes the data employed and the ways in which poverty and deprivation are measured, and as background to the present study summarises the overall national results on poverty and deprivation discussed in detail in Callan et al., (1996). Chapter 4 repeats with the 1994 survey data our earlier survey-based analysis for 1987 (Nolan, Whelan and Williams, 1994), to see the extent to which poverty has become more concentrated over time in particular types of geographical area, in particular forms of housing tenure, or in some combinations of type of area and housing tenure. We then extend that analysis in Chapters 5 and 6 to explore what lies behind the observed changes over time, and to assess the extent to which variation in the risk of poverty by location and tenure type can be accounted for by factors such as social class, education, labour force status and labour market experience.

Chapter 7 then looks at variation in poverty risk and incidence in the household surveys by planning region. Chapter 8 makes use of the detailed data in the 1986 and 1991 Censuses of Population Small

Area Population Statistics (SAPs) to examine the spatial distribution of unemployment, unskilled manual social class and local authority rented housing. Finally, Chapter 9 brings together the conclusions.

Chapter 2

Arguments for Spatial Intervention

Before turning to the analysis of survey and Census data from a spatial perspective, it is useful to outline the various arguments which have been advanced for adopting such a perspective. One obvious reason for doing so is that area-based strategies have become a central part of public policy aimed at combating poverty. However, it is necessary to keep in mind that, while a variety of area-based initiatives have emerged in recent years, only the partnership arrangements which emerged from the Programme for Economic and Social Progress (PESP) have had a specific remit to target disadvantaged groups (Walsh, 1996).

The argument outlined in *Strategies for the Nineties* (NESC, 1990) was that general measures to improve employment creation would not be sufficient to have an impact on those experiencing long-term unemployment. Special employment measures were required which would be "targeted in an integrated fashion in the context of local area-based strategies". Increased polarisation and its spatial manifestation, provided an important component of the rationale for spatial interventions.

> "The concentrated incidence of unemployment, low incomes, and deprivation in certain communities and regions gives a *prima facie* case for developing area-based programmes." (NESC, 1990)

The Council also argued that intensive co-ordinated spatial interventions containing elements of housing and environmental improvements as well as retraining and employment schemes, could have an impact over and above their separate effects. Furthermore, it was held that participation of local communities in the planning and delivery of area-based projects would help ensure that they more accurately reflected local needs and priorities.

The PESP Area-based Response which was initiated in twelve areas had as its objective to establish an "integrated approach to implementing a community response in particular local areas to long-term unemployment and the danger of long-term unemployment". Craig and McKeown (1994: xiii) sets out the more detailed objectives which were contained in the guidelines issued to the partnerships:

- To work with people who are long-term unemployed and those in danger of becoming long-term unemployed in order to improve their skills and self-confidence, their involvement in the community and to increase their opportunities of getting a job or starting their own business

- To promote the fundamental attitude change needed to enable individuals to generate enterprise thereby creating additional employment and to encourage a more positive attitude towards the recruitment of people who are long-term unemployed

- To work at the local level to generate more jobs through sustainable enterprises and through the promotion of local economic projects and initiatives which stimulate confidence and investment.

Craig and McKeown note that the interpretation of these objectives at local level within each of the twelve partnerships led to a diversity of approaches and a variety of actions.

The area-based interventions thus involved application of the three geographical dimensions referred to by Walsh (1996):

- Targeting of resources ("positive spatial discrimination")

- Co-ordination of services ("local planning")

- Economic and social regeneration.

While the PESP area-based initiatives had many dimensions, Craig and McKeown (1994) in their evaluation of the programme concluded that it was "designed as a means of ensuring that one area is favoured over another". The manner by which one seeks to achieve this objective will be determined by what one considers the appropriate balance of targeting, participation and development activities. It will also be affected by the relative emphasis that one places on processes operating within a local area which increase the likelihood of deprivation and processes which while having nothing to do with the area *per se* lead to the people who are deprived being concentrated in particular locations. Thus, as Pringle (1996) notes, the first includes factors such as poor infrastructure while the second includes migration and the filtering effects of the housing market.

There are in fact a variety of different grounds on which a focus on the spatial distribution of poverty might be justified:

- The most straightforward justification is based on the fact that if poor households are highly concentrated in specific areas then it is possible to target resources on those areas in order to maximise the number of households reached.

- An alternative justification could be premised on the notion that interventions involving an increased commitment, and improved co-ordination, of resources are of particular relevance in highly disadvantaged areas because of the cumulative and multi-dimensional nature of the deprivation to which they are exposed.

- While a particular justification for targeted intervention does not necessarily involve a commitment to an explicit understanding of the pattern of causation leading to spatial concentration of disadvantage; almost inevitably, some such set of assumptions underlies most interventions. A variety of positions can exist. It is possible to see spatial concentration of deprivation as having no causal significance or distinctive consequences. Instead concentration could be seen to arise simply as a consequence of differences in other genuinely causal variables such as human capital. Administrative policies could be seen as exacerbating such tendencies. On the other hand, location could be thought to play a potentially independent role in a number of ways. Employers' hiring behaviour could mean that merely residing at a particular address could increase one's risk of unemployment and poverty at a given level of human capital. More broadly, those coming from areas where the resource stock in terms of access to training, education, financial institutions etc. is poor could be seen as additionally disadvantaged. Much more controversially, at the centre of recent debates concerning the creation of a spatially concentrated underclass is the (highly contested) idea that persistent poverty is transmitted across generations through a fundamental altering of norms and 'tastes' in relation to welfare dependency, chronic joblessness, or non-marital fertility (Nolan and Whelan, 1996).

- Finally, it might be argued that poverty "black spots" could produce a qualitatively different experience of poverty in terms of factors such as physical and mental health, degree of economic strain and alienation from social and political life ranging from social

contacts to church attendance and participation and confidence in
the political process.

It is far from easy to deduce the particular understanding that un-
derlay the PESP area-based initiatives. NESC (1993: 417), in wel-
coming the extension of the scheme, noted that the National Development Plan envisaged an extended programme of local development
targeted at disadvantaged areas and a broadening of the nature of
the programme to focus on such factors as early school leaving:

> "This broader focus is particularly welcomed since it addresses the
> nature of cumulative disadvantage which generates and sustains
> local exclusion. It is this localised process of interaction between
> labour market, education, housing and environmental factors
> which is most likely to be addressed effectively by an area-based
> strategy." (NESC, 1993: 417)

This position is consistent with one which sees locational features as
a crucial ingredient in producing cumulative disadvantage. But, in
fact, as Walsh (1996) notes, area-based initiatives have not tended to
involve investment in such areas as the physical fabric of poor areas
but have tended to focus on developing human capacity and business
development where the possibility exists of subsequent mobility out
of the area. While the deprivation profile of areas may remain relatively constant over time it is necessary to remember that we are
highly unlikely to be dealing with the same households or individuals. The strategies adopted have been varied, and have included
direct attempts to reduce discriminatory behaviour on the part of
employers. However, the available literature suggests that the main
thrust of the interventions has not in fact derived from a conception
of accumulating disadvantages and vicious circle processes arising
from concentrations of disadvantage. Rather, areas seem to be con-
ceived as the sites in which the consequences of wider processes are
expressed and the specific resources associated with interventions
are

> "designed to increase the effectiveness of mainstream programme
> spending which each public agency will be required to identify in
> respect of each designated area." (NESC, 1993: 417)

The superior effectiveness of a decentralised approach now appears to
be crucial and partnership, participation and planning become key

concepts, as in the Global Grant (1994) which covers the continued support of the twelve PESP area-based interventions and a variety of local development groups (NESC, 1994: 126, Haase et al., 1996: 2).

Such an approach is, of course, consistent with an explicit focus on areas of high socio-economic disadvantage. The integration and co-ordination of existing services on the basis of partnership arrange-ments may be seen as of particular value in areas where deprivation takes a multidimensional form. More recent discussions of commu-nity development have attempted to develop the argument that in-volvement of local communities in the process of economic and social regeneration has an intrinsic value; and that rather than being pe-ripheral to processes of economic change it is a crucial means by which marginalised groups can come to share in the benefits of eco-nomic progress. Community development as a process is seen to be diminished in the absence of a commitment to tackling disadvantage (ADM, 1994). Frazer (1996) links the argument for community devel-opment initiatives to the failure of trickle down policies to prevent the emergence of growing concentrations of poverty and to the oppor-tunity to use resources in a more integrated manner. However, in ad-dition to arguments relating to effectiveness and efficiency his case for empowerment is based on an understanding of social exclusion which recognises that loss of skills, self confidence and motivation are crucial elements of the process.[1]

However, within the context of a heightened localism and the emergence of community as an "official" actor in development initia-tives and programmes (Curtin, 1996: 248) the argument has emerged that it is necessary to "distinguish clearly between the idea of an area-based approach and the idea of a selective approach" (NESC, 1994:91). In turn, the extent to which poverty is concentrated in par-ticular areas and the merits of an area-based approach to long-term unemployment and disadvantage become distinct questions. From this perspective the interesting issues relating to local partnerships are seen to concern the links between local and national partnership arrangements and the need for mediating arrangements, the limits to centralised policy making, and the extent to which "democratic ex-perimentalism" is a form of intervention which is particularly equipped to develop the kind of flexible and innovative response which current forms of flexible production demand (OECD, 1996). Those more sceptical about the value of area-based responses as a general strategy have gone as far as to question whether they involve

---

[1] See also Rourke (1994).

a journey "back to the future" (Curtin, 1996), in that the urge towards community is nothing new on the Irish scene although more recent interventions have largely neglected the early literature on community development (Shortall, 1994). A longer term perspective raises a variety of issues regarding the use of terms such as "community" and "partnership", the distribution of benefits and systems of governance. Thus the appropriate role of local government has become a particularly tendentious issue and even the OECD (1996) analysis — which deliberately chose to focus on the most successful variants of area-based intervention — laid particular emphasis on the instability of the arrangements and the manner in which this instability is directly connected to questions regarding the democratic legitimacy of the partnerships (Coyle, 1996; FitzGerald and Keegan 1993; NESC, 1994: 131–139; OECD, 1996: 85).

Chapter 3

Data and Measurement of Poverty at Household Level

Introduction

We now turn to the empirical analysis using household survey data. In this chapter the two surveys 1987 and 1994 are described and the approach adopted to measure poverty and deprivation discussed. The picture at national level, from the results for 1987 and 1994, is summarised as background to the present study. These results are presented in detail in Callan et al., (1989 and 1996). The chapter goes on to describe the information available in the surveys which provide a window into spatial aspects of poverty, to be employed in the subsequent analysis. Finally, there is a summary of the points made in the chapter.

The Household Survey Data

The household data sets employed in this study are the 1987 Survey of Income Distribution, Poverty and Usage of State Services and the 1994 Living in Ireland Survey, each carried out by the Economic and Social Research Institute. Both were designed to provide a national representative sample of the population resident in private households. Full descriptions are in Callan et al., (1989) and (1994) respectively, and only a brief outline will be given here.

The 1987 Survey of Income Distribution, Poverty and Usage of State Services used the Register of Electors as a sampling frame, and obtained responses from a sample of 3,294 households. The effective response rate was 64% of valid addresses contacted, comparable to surveys such as the Central Statistics Office's Household Budget Surveys. The sample for analysis has been re-weighted to correct for non-response and for the over-representation of large households produced by an individual-based sampling frame, using external information from the much larger Labour Force Survey. The variables

used for re-weighting are the number of adults in the household, ur-
ban/rural location, age and socio-economic group of the household.
The representativeness of the sample has been validated by comparison with a variety of other sources of information, such as the Census
of Population, administrative statistics on numbers in receipt of
social welfare and Revenue Commissioners' data on taxable incomes.

The 1994 Living in Ireland Survey was the first wave of the Irish
element of the European Community Household Panel (ECHP) carried out for Eurostat, the Statistical Office of the European Community, by the ESRI. The survey also used the Electoral Register as
sampling frame, and obtained information for 4,048 households,
62.5% of valid addresses contacted. Once again the sample for analysis was re-weighted to accord with the Labour Force Survey in terms
of key household characteristics. The sample has been validated in
terms of composition by age, sex and marital status and numbers in
receipt of social welfare, and appears to represent the population well
in respect of these variables.

Both household surveys obtained detailed information on the income of household members from different sources, on the nature of
their participation in the labour force, and on a number of other features relating to both individuals and their households. This includes
information on whether the household has or is able to avail of a
range of items or activities, which can be used to complement income
in measuring poverty and deprivation and is described in the next
section. For the present study information on the household which
allows a spatial perspective to be adopted is of central importance,
and the nature of this information in these surveys is discussed on
page 15. First, the measurement of poverty at national level and results on that basis from the 1987 and 1994 surveys are discussed.

Measuring Poverty and Deprivation

We have discussed extensively elsewhere the many issues of definition and measurement which arise in seeking to measure poverty
(most recently in Callan et al., (1996), Chapter 2). Without repeating
that discussion, we take as our starting-point for the present study
that the concept of poverty adopted is an explicitly relative one,
relating to exclusion from the ordinary life of society due to lack of
resources. We continue to stress, as in previous work, the importance
of acknowledging uncertainty and absence of robustness in results.
We therefore employ several different relative income poverty lines,

and a measure which takes into account both income and non-monetary indicators of deprivation.

Relative income poverty lines are calculated as a particular percentage of average household income, taking differences in household size and composition into account. We take into account the fact that adults have greater needs than children and that there are economies of scale in consumption by using equivalence scales to adjust household income. Here we report results employing an equivalence scale of 0.66 for additional adults and 0.33 for children. The two relative income lines employed in this study are 50 and 60 per cent of mean equivalent household disposable income. For an adult living alone, this produced poverty lines in 1994 of about £65 and £77 per week. The corresponding poverty lines derived from average income in 1987 were £43 and £51 respectively.[1]

Reliance on income alone is open to the criticism that it may not be a good measure of low consumption and therefore of deprivation. If poverty is defined as exclusion from the ordinary life of society due to lack of resources — understood as a state of generalised deprivation — it should be characterised by both a low standard of consumption and a low level of income. It may then be necessary to employ both a consumption/deprivation and an income criterion in identifying the poor (Callan, Nolan and Whelan, 1993, Nolan and Whelan, 1996). Our analysis of life-style deprivation indicators in the 1987 ESRI survey enabled us to identify three distinct dimensions, and the one crucial to our current concerns we termed *basic deprivation*. This comprises a set of eight indicators (see Table 3.2) which relate to the enforced absence of such items as food, clothing and heat and going into debt to meet ordinary living expenses. The analysis showed that these items reflected rather basic aspects of current material deprivation, represent socially defined necessities, are possessed by most people, are considered as necessities by most people and cluster together, lending support to the notion that they are useful as indicators of underlying generalised deprivation. The combined income and deprivation standard employed here is that a household is counted as poor where it reports enforced lack of at least one of these basic items

---

[1] Full details of the calculation of the relative income lines, and of the consequences of varying the equivalence scales, is in Callan et al., (1996).

and falls below 60 per cent of mean income.[2] This combined measure is the one which we feel best captures our underlying conceptualisation of poverty as involving enforced absence of socially defined necessities. In the current context it is important to stress that unlike items such as cars, telephones and holidays there is no evidence for significant urban-rural differences in the extent to which the items included in the basic deprivation index are considered to be necessities (Nolan and Whelan, 1996: 79–80).

The National Pattern of Poverty and Deprivation in 1987 and 1994

Detailed results from the application of relative income poverty lines to the 1987 and 1994 data were presented in Callan et al., 1989 and 1996 respectively, but it is worth briefly summarising the overall picture here. Table 3.1 shows the percentage of households and persons falling below the 50 and 60 per cent relative income lines (with the equivalence scale 1.0/0.66/0.33 as described earlier) in each year. About one in five persons were below the 50 per cent line, and one in three below the 60 per cent line, in 1994. The percentage of persons below the 50 per cent but more particularly the 60 per cent line rose between 1987 and 1994, although analysis of income poverty gaps, which describe the "depth" of poverty, shows that those below these income lines were considerably closer to them in 1994 than in 1987 (see Callan et al., 1994, Chapter 4). Results with alternative equivalence scales (1/0.6/0.4; 1/0.7/0.5) showed a similar overall pattern. Average household income rose rapidly during the period 1987–1994, unlike the preceding seven years, so a substantial fall was seen in the numbers falling below poverty lines remaining constant in real terms.

---

[2] This approach is open to the criticism that it may fail to consider changing standards in relation to what are societally defined standards. However, for the time period for which we are concerned (10 years) this is unlikely to be a significant problem. The 60 per cent income line was chosen on the basis of an earlier analysis of the labour force situation and life-style characteristics of those falling between a range of poverty lines. Exclusion of those between the 50 and 60 per cent lines who are experiencing basic deprivation would involve defining as non-poor a set of households whose profile appears to be consistent with experiencing *enforced* basic deprivation (Nolan and Whelan, 1996: 124–26). The choice of any income line inevitably involves judgement; however, we are of the opinion that our joint income-deprivation measure is, if anything, too restrictive rather than too generous.

Table 3.1: Percentage of Persons Below Relative Income Poverty Lines, 1987 and 1994

	(Equivalence Scale A — 1.0/0.66/0.33)	
	1987	1994
Percentage of households below line:		
50 per cent line	16.3	18.5
60 per cent line	28.5	34.6
Percentage of persons below line:		
50 per cent line	18.9	20.7
60 per cent line	29.8	34.0

Significant changes in the composition of the households below the relative income lines took place between 1987 and 1994, as documented in Callan et al., (1996). The most striking changes were the increase in risk facing single-adult households, older people, female-headed households and those headed by someone working full-time in the home — with a good deal of overlap between these groups. The risk of income poverty fell substantially for farm households, because the year covered by the 1987 survey was a particularly bad one for income from agriculture and there was sustained growth in farm incomes over the period. Households with an unemployed head remained at high risk and comprised one-third or more of those below the relative income lines; there was also a high level of risk for households with large numbers of children and lone parent households.

As well as household income, non-monetary indicators of deprivation have also been employed in attempting to identify those in the 1987 and 1994 surveys who were experiencing exclusion from ordinary living patterns due to lack of resources. Analysis of available indicators identified eight basic indicators, relating to what households considered to be enforced absence of food, clothing and heat and going into debt to meet ordinary living expenses, as the most useful in this context, (see Table 3.2). The combined income and deprivation standard employed here is that a household is counted as poor where it reports enforced lack of at least one of these basic items and falls below 60 per cent of mean income. About 16 per cent of households in the 1987 sample were in that position. By 1994, the percentage had fallen marginally, to 15 per cent. Comparing the households in that

situation in 1994 with those simply falling below half average income, about 10 per cent of all households would be identified as poor
by both approaches, but the extent of divergence between the two
groups means that applying both approaches and comparing the results is of considerable value. Households with an unemployed head
remain the most substantial group among the poor when a combination of income and deprivation information is used.

Table 3.2 shows the items which are in fact lacked by those experiencing basic deprivation and having an income below the 50 per
cent and the 60 per cent lines in 1987 and 1994. The percentage
lacking specific items is in some cases higher in 1994 than in 1987
and in some cases lower, but the overall pattern is quite similar in
the two years. In 1994, over half the households below the 50 per cent
line and experiencing basic deprivation had severe debt problems,
about 40 per cent said they could not afford two pairs of shoes, and
the same number said they could not afford a roast or equivalent once
a week.

Some key factors underlying the observed changes in the extent
and nature of poverty at national level have been identified in Callan
et al., (1996), though further research is required to tease out a more
complete picture. As well as the persistence of long-term unemployment, one of the most important factors was the evolution of social
welfare rates for different types of recipient. In particular, the policy
priority of increasing rates to what were the lowest-paying schemes
at the beginning of the period contributed to reducing poverty gaps
for those relying on, for example, Unemployment Assistance and
Supplementary Welfare Allowance. However, it also meant that the
elderly received increases which lagged behind average incomes
(though keeping ahead of the increase in consumer prices), so their
poverty risk rose.

Table 3.2: Nature of Basic Deprivation for Households at Different Income Levels and Lacking at Least One Basic Item, 1987 and 1994 Samples

	Households Experiencing Basic Deprivation and			
	Below the 50% line		Between the 50% and 60% lines	
	% lacking item			
	1987	1994	1987	1994
Debt	54.5	56.9	44.0	33.2
Went without main meal	17.0	23.4	13.8	17.3
Went without heat	27.4	46.6	23.7	38.1
Enforced lack of:				
New clothes	33.6	38.3	22.3	41.4
Two pairs of shoes	43.7	33.9	36.2	37.2
Warm overcoat	24.4	28.5	31.7	25.7
Roast or equivalent once a week	44.7	38.4	37.2	33.3
Meal with meat, fish or equivalent	39.3	24.1	29.7	21.4

Taking a Spatial Perspective on Poverty and Deprivation in the Household Surveys

Both the 1987 Survey of Income Distribution, Poverty and Usage of State Services and the 1994 Living in Ireland Survey were designed to provide a national representative sample of the population resident in private households. While the number of households in the achieved samples, at 3,294 in 1987 and 4,048 in 1994 is relatively large, the extent to which the results can be disaggregated by geographical area is limited by both sample size and the sampling design. Thus while it would be possible to derive poverty rates by county from the samples it would not be productive to do so: analysis at the level of planning region, each consisting of a number of counties, is more reliable and is carried out in Chapter 7. First, however, we make use of a household location variable, available in both surveys, relating to the *type* of area in which the household is located, as well as a measure of the nature of the household's housing tenure. We make use of the tenure variable because it is reasonable to expect that urban local authority housing, and in particular rented local authority housing, will account for a large proportion of concentrated pockets of poverty. In establishing the extent to which the poor are located in such households we will provide one estimate of the extent to which poverty is spatially concentrated.[3]

Interviewers classified the location of each household as falling into one of twelve categories which in the bulk of our analysis have been aggregated as follows.

1. Open Country

2. Village/Town <3,000

3. Town >3,000

4. Waterford, Cork, Galway and Limerick cities

5. Dublin city and county.

As far as tenure is concerned, respondents were asked which of the following categories described their household's tenure arrangements:

1. Property owned outright

2. Property owned with mortgage

3. Local authority tenant purchaser

4. Local authority rented accommodation

5. Private rented accommodation.

Each of these variables serves as a spatially relevant indicator, used separately and in combination for this purpose in analysis of the 1987 survey in Nolan, Whelan and Williams (1994). They will be employed in the next chapter to assess variation in poverty risks and concentration of poverty in both 1987 and 1994.

---

[3] Such a measure will not capture spatial concentration associated with small farming or rural unemployment. On the other hand, it will include poor local authority households which do not form part of a spatially concentrated set of poor households.

Conclusions

This chapter has described the 1987 and 1994 household surveys to be employed in subsequent chapters and the approach to measuring poverty and deprivation to be adopted. As in our previous research, both relative income poverty lines and a combination of these lines with non-monetary deprivation indicators will be used. Survey-based results at a national level already published show an increase in the proportion of persons falling below relative income lines between 1987 and 1994, although they did not fall as far below these lines on average in the latter year. The percentage both below the relative income lines and experiencing basic deprivation has fallen marginally over the period. Some notable changes in the types of household below the poverty lines also took place. These changes at national level provide the background against which the spatial pattern of poverty and deprivation will be studied. While the household surveys cannot be used to derive poverty rates for county level or below, they can serve as the basis for analysis of the relationships between type of area, tenure, and poverty, on which we embark in the next chapter.

Chapter 4

Poverty by Area and Tenure Type

Introduction

Using the 1994 and 1987 surveys, we first present in this chapter results for poverty risk and incidence by area type, then the corresponding results by tenure type, and then combine area and tenure
type. The analysis of the spatial distribution of poverty which follows
is part of a wider study of processes of social exclusion in which we
are involved. In subsequent publications we will present detailed statistical results relating to changes between 1987 and 1994; relating
not only to the overall effect of spatial variables but to their partial
impact when other related variables have been taken into account.
Here we aim for a more informal presentation and the interpretation
of our results will be directed not by the statistical significance of any
difference taken in isolation but by evidence of substantial changes in
the pattern of results across time.

Poverty and Deprivation by Area Type

We saw in the previous chapter that in both the 1987 and 1994 surveys households can be categorised by the *type* of area in which they
are located. In order to have sufficient numbers in each (particularly
when we go on to cross-classify type and tenure), we combine the
twelve categories employed in the questionnaire into five: "open country", "village or town with population of less than 3,000", "town with
population of 3,000 or over", "Cork, Limerick, Waterford or Galway
city", and "Dublin city or county". In Table 4.1 we examine the manner in which the *risk*[1] of poverty varies across such areas and how the

---

[1] We use the term risk to refer to the probability of being poor i.e. the risk
of poverty measures the proportion of a group which falls below an income
line, providing an assessment of the degree to which that group is at risk of
poverty.

patterns for 1987 and 1994 compare, with all three poverty standards used.

In 1994 the highest risk of poverty for all three poverty lines was in villages and towns with populations of less than three thousand.[2] For the income lines the lowest rate was observed in Dublin. For the combined measure, however, the figure for open country households was significantly lower than for any other location. In 1987, Dublin had a relatively low poverty risk by all three standards, though the differential was least with the combined income and deprivation measure. The overall household poverty rate increased between 1987 and 1994 with both the 50 and 60 per cent lines, but here it is the spatial pattern which is of interest. With the 50 per cent poverty line, there was little change in the case of open country, villages and towns with populations less than three thousand, and for the main urban centres other than Dublin. For towns with populations in excess of three thousand the rate increased from 14 to 20 per cent, and for Dublin the rate rose from less than 9 to 15 per cent. For the 60 per cent relative income line there was a rise in the rate of poverty for each area type, but the increase was most pronounced for towns and villages with populations of less than three thousand — from 37 to 47 per cent — and for Dublin — from 17 to 27 per cent.

In contrast to the relative income lines, when we focus on the combined income and deprivation measure the overall poverty rate declined from 16 to 15 per cent. The most substantial decline was for households located in open country, where the rate fell from 16 to 10 per cent. The rates for villages, towns and the four cities outside Dublin were not very different in 1994 to those observed in 1987. The exception is Dublin, where the rate increased from 12 to 15 per cent. The decline in the poverty rate for those in open country using this combined income and deprivation measure, when it was rising for other area types, is reflected in substantial differences between urban and rural areas in the extent of basic deprivation in 1994. For households below the 60 per cent relative income line, the average score was higher in urban than in rural areas for most of the indicators in the basic index, and the overall average score on that index was just over 2 in rural areas compared with 3 in urban areas.

While the magnitude of the change varies across the poverty standards, the relative position of Dublin, with distinctively low poverty rates in 1987, deteriorates across all three poverty lines. This con-

---

[2] For a recent treatment of rural poverty see Curtin, Haase and Tovey (eds.), 1996.

tributes to a narrowing of differentials between areas. Villages and towns with populations of less than three thousand had the highest rate of poverty for all three poverty standards at both points in time, and Dublin city and county had the lowest, but by 1994, in relation to the income lines, it is the homogeneity of poverty rates rather than the extent of variation which is striking. This is consistent with the substantial decline in the risk of poverty for farming households described elsewhere (Callan et al., 1996). However, there are clearly other factors operating, since differentials between Dublin and *all* other locations narrowed rather than only *vis-à-vis* open country; this is an issue to which we shall return. A slightly different outcome is observed for the combined income and deprivation measure. Here a substantial absolute reduction in the rate of poverty for open country widens the gap between this location and all others. Otherwise, however, variation by area remains relatively modest.

Table 4.1: Risk of Poverty by Type of Area for 1987 and 1994

	50% Income Line		60% Income Line		60% Income Line and Basic Deprivation	
	1987	1994	1987	1994	1987	1994
Area:	*Per Cent of Households*					
Open Country	21.6	19.6	34.7	37.4	15.5	9.6
Village/Town <3,000	25.2	26.4	36.9	46.5	23.6	21.7
Town > 3,000	14.2	19.7	31.5	37.2	18.1	18.7
Waterford, Cork, Galway and Limerick cities	18.0	18.4	28.0	32.0	21.0	19.2
Dublin city and county	8.7	15.1	16.7	27.4	12.0	19.2
All	17.0	18.9	29.1	34.8	16.4	14.9

In Table 4.2 we turn from the risk to the *incidence* of poverty — i.e. the percentage of all poor people who are located in each type of area. The pattern of change between 1987 and 1994 is straightforward. For each of the poverty standards the percentage of households below the relative poverty lines found in open country areas decreased substantially, while the total number of households in such areas declined only slightly. This was balanced by a marked increase in the percentage of the poor who were located in Dublin, when the percentage of all households in Dublin increased only slightly. The proportion of poor households located in Dublin in 1994 is still at most only as great as its share in the population — in 1987 Dublin was under-represented among the poor. Correspondingly, the relative income lines suggest that open country areas had significantly more than their "share" of poor households in 1987 and about the same proportion of the poor as of all households in 1994. The combined income and deprivation standard suggests that in 1987 these areas had about their share of the poor but were significantly underrepresented by 1994. It is villages and towns with populations of less than three thousand which emerge as consistently containing more poor households than one would expect simply on the basis of their share in the population.

Table 4.2: Incidence of Poverty by Type of Area for 1987 and 1994

	50% Income Line		60% Income Line		60% Income Line and Basic Deprivation		Percentage of All Households	
	1987	1994	1987	1994	1987	1994	1987	1994
Area:	Per Cent of Households							
Open Country	46.5	34.3	42.7	35.6	33.9	21.3	35.8	33.1
Village/ Town <3,000	16.7	14.7	14.3	14.1	16.2	15.1	11.2	10.0
Town >3,000	15.1	19.0	19.5	19.4	19.8	22.8	18.0	18.1
Waterford, Cork, Galway and Limerick cities	9.1	8.5	8.3	8.0	11.0	11.3	8.6	8.7
Dublin city and county	13.5	23.5	15.1	22.9	19.2	29.5	26.3	29.5
All	100.0	100.0	100.0	100.0	100.0	100.0	100.0	100.0

Poverty and Deprivation by Tenure Type

One of the limitations of the analysis we have conducted up to this point is that it is perfectly possible that a more detailed disaggregation would reveal pockets of deprivation within the areas we have been able to distinguish. We deal with this in two ways. Later we will make use of the Census SAPS data which will allow us to look at much smaller areas. This further disaggregation, however, must be bought at the price of forfeiting the richness of household data available in our surveys. The second, complementary strategy is to make use of other information in the household surveys which tells us more about the area, or type of area, in which the household is located. We now focus on the extent to which poverty is associated with the nature of the household's housing tenure, and in the next section bring tenure and area type together.

In Table 4.3 we look at the variation in risk level across these types of tenure for each of our three poverty standards in 1987 and 1994. In 1987 the tenure types fell into three groups in terms of poverty risk. Owners with a mortgage had particularly low poverty rates, of 7 per cent at the 50 per cent income line, 13 per cent at the 60 per cent line and 6 per cent at the combined poverty lines. At the other extreme, local authority renters had very high poverty rates with these three standards, of 37 per cent, 59 per cent and 47 per cent respectively. The remaining tenure types — outright owners, local authority tenant purchasers and private renters — had intermediate levels of poverty risks, which were at least half those facing local authority tenants but 2.5 to 3 times those of the mortgage holders.

By 1994 a number of changes had occurred. For the income poverty lines the overall poverty rates for the sample rose between 1987 and 1994, and this was reflected in an increase in risk for all tenure types. Local authority renters saw a relatively rapid increase in risk and are at much the highest risk in 1994, with half that group below the 50 per cent line, and three-quarters below the 60 per cent line. At the 60 per cent income line local authority tenant purchasers saw the most rapid increase (in proportionate terms) in risk over the period, from 28 to 42 per cent. At the combined income/deprivation standard the overall poverty rate fell marginally, as did the risk for house owners and those in private rented accommodation. Even with this standard, however, the risk for local authority tenants and local authority tenant purchasers rose. For local authority renters the increase was from 47 to 52 per cent, while for local authority purchasers it was even greater, from 15 to 25 per cent. By 1994, there is a consistent ranking of tenure types by risk across the three poverty standards. Local authority tenants have what are, by any standard, strikingly high poverty rates. They are followed at some distance by local authority purchasers and then by those in private rented accommodation, while home owners and, in particular, mortgage holders, display the lowest rates.

Table 4.3: Risk of Poverty by Tenure Type for 1987 and 1994

	50% Income Line		60% Income Line		60% Income Line and Basic Deprivation	
	1987	1994	1987	1994	1987	1994
	Per Cent					
Owned Outright	16.8	18.1	30.0	37.8	12.6	10.5
Owned with Mortgage	6.7	8.7	2.5	14.6	6.3	5.5
Local Authority Tenant Purchase	17.8	21.8	27.5	41.6	15.1	24.5
Local Authority Rented	37.4	49.8	59.1	74.6	46.8	52.0
Other Rented	14.4	15.1	27.7	34.0	21.3	15.3
All	17.0	18.8	29.1	34.6	16.4	14.9

Turning to the incidence or concentration of poverty by tenure type, this depends on both the risk levels for each type of tenure and the distribution of households across tenure types. From Table 4.4, we can see that change in the distribution of households across tenure types between 1987 and 1994, was relatively modest. There were small increases in the proportion owning with a mortgage or renting privately, with falls in the proportion of outright owners and local authority tenants or tenant-purchasers. What is then striking is how little the incidence of poverty across tenure types has changed. Households which are owned outright generally become a little less important among the poor, and those owned with a mortgage or private rented become more important, but the changes are not great. Those in rented local authority housing make up a slightly smaller proportion of the poor in 1994 than in 1987 with all three poverty standards,[3] while tenant-purchasers in local authority housing increased as a proportion of the poor with the combined income and deprivation standard. Taking both renters and tenant-purchasers together, poverty did not become further concentrated to any great extent in local authority housing between 1987 and 1994. Such

---

[3] Given that risk levels for these groups rose over that period, this is obviously due to the decline in numbers in such housing.

households were indeed exposed to very high risk levels, but even for the combined income and life-style deprivation line, where concentration is most evident, almost one in two poor households was outside local authority housing in both years.[4]

Table 4.4: Incidence of Poverty by Tenure Type for 1987 and 1994

	50% Income Line		60% Income Line		60% Income Line and Basic Deprivation		Percentage of all Households	
	1987	1994	1987	1994	1987	1994	1987	1994
	Per Cent							
Owned Outright	44.2	40.5	45.9	45.9	34.0	29.4	44.4	42.0
Owned with Mortgage	11.1	14.8	12.2	13.5	10.8	11.8	28.1	32.0
Local Authority Tenant Purchase	8.1	7.3	7.3	7.6	7.1	10.2	7.7	6.3
Local Authority Tenant	32.1	30.9	29.6	25.1	41.3	40.4	14.5	11.7
Other Rented	4.5	6.5	5.0	7.9	6.8	8.2	5.2	8.0
All	100.0	100.0	100.0	100.0	100.0	100.0	100.0	100.0

Combining Area Type and Tenure

We now bring together the survey information on type of area and housing tenure to look at their combined effects. For ease of presentation we focus on local authority housing versus all other tenure types, and on the combined income and deprivation poverty standard. (As we have seen, this standard produces a higher degree of concentration of the poor in local authority housing than the income lines alone.) Table 4.5 shows the risk of poverty in 1987 and 1994 by area type and local authority/other on this basis. In 1987, those in local authority housing had a poverty risk of about 36 per cent on average, and this did not vary greatly by area type except for villages and towns of under 3,000, where the figure was a good deal higher at 52 per cent. The risk of poverty for households in private housing was

---

[4] If one focuses on the relative income lines, this figure rises to almost two out of three.

much lower on average at 11 per cent, but in this case the striking exception was the much lower risk facing such households in Dublin, where the figure was only 4 per cent. While those in local authority housing were thus on average about 3.3 times more likely to be poor than other households, the differential for Dublin was about 7.5:1.

Table 4.5: Risk of Poverty Using the 60% Income Line Plus Basic Deprivation by Area and Tenure Type for 1987 and 1994

	Local Authority	*Other*	*Local Authority*	*Other*
	1987		*1994*	
	Per Cent			
Open Country	32.8	14.0	17.5	9.2
Village/Town: <3,000	52.0	12.0	47.5	12.6
Town: >3,000	31.2	11.8	39.9	13.0
Waterford, Cork, Galway and Limerick cities	37.0	11.2	44.1	6.7
Dublin city and county	32.9	4.4	47.3	5.6
All	35.8	10.9	42.4	9.0

Between 1987 and 1994, the risk of poverty using the combined income/deprivation standard increased for those in local authority housing from 36 per cent to 42 per cent, while it declined for other households from 11 to 9 per cent. The differential in risk between these two tenure groups overall had thus risen to 4.7 by 1994. However, there are important differences in trend across area types. The risk of poverty declined sharply for those in open country, whether in local authority housing or — like most such households — in private housing. Those in local authority housing in villages and towns with populations of less than 3,000 saw a smaller drop in the poverty rate from its relatively high 1987 figure of 52 percent to 48 per cent. In all other areas, there was a substantial increase in the risk of poverty for those in local authority housing. This increase was greatest in Dublin, where the poverty risk for local authority housing climbs from 33 to 47 per cent. For those outside local authority housing, risk fell not only for open country areas but also for cities outside Dublin. The disparity in risk between local authority and private housing in Dublin is now even greater than in 1987, reaching 8.4:1. For the other main cities the corresponding figure is 6:1 while elsewhere it is a good deal lower.

It is worth noting a further distinctive feature of the situation in urban centres, not shown in the table but revealed by distinguishing between local authority purchasers and tenants. Outside the urban centres, the poverty rate for local authority renting households is 1.5–2 times that of tenant–purchasers. In the urban centres, however, the gap is wider at 3:1. The poverty rate for those renting local authority housing in Dublin is 67 per cent, and for the other urban centres the figure is 56 per cent: in terms of a housing/area type disaggregation, these are the highest poverty rates in the country.

In Table 4.6 we look at the same breakdown as Table 4.5, but from the point of view of incidence rather than risk. Overall, as we have seen, about half the poor were in local authority housing in both 1987 and 1994. However, there were some important changes in the way these were distributed by area type. The proportion of poor households in open country, both private and local authority, fell sharply, while the proportion in Dublin rose for both tenure types. By 1994, 21 per cent of the poor were in local authority housing in Dublin, while 9 per cent were in Dublin private housing. (Whereas Dublin contained one-third of all local authority households in 1987, it had only 29 per cent of poor local authority households; by 1994 it had 37 per cent of all local authority households but 42 per cent of those in poverty.) In terms of concentration, thus, combining area type and tenure allows us to see that one in five poor households is in local authority housing in Dublin, 30 per cent are in public housing in one of the five cities including Dublin, and in total 40 per cent are in public housing in a town of over 3,000 persons. Conversely, a clear majority of the poor are not in urban public housing.

Table 4.6: Incidence of Poverty Using 60% Income Line Plus Basic Deprivation by Area and Tenure Type for 1987 and 1994 (Percentage of Total Households in Parentheses)

	Local Authority		Other		Local Authority		Other	
	1987				*1994*			
	Per cent							
Open Country	5.9	(2.9)	28.0	(32.7)	1.9	(1.6)	19.4	(31.5)
Village/Town <3,000	10.3	(3.4)	5.8	(8.2)	8.6	(2.7)	6.4	(7.7)
Town >3,000	11.1	(5.7)	8.7	(12.3)	10.3	(3.9)	12.5	(14.2)
Waterford, Cork, Galway and Limerick cities	7.3	(3.2)	3.6	(5.2)	8.6	(3.0)	2.7	(5.8)
Dublin city and county	14.0	(7.3)	5.1	(19.2)	21.0	(6.7)	8.6	(22.8)
All	48.7	(22.4)	51.3	(77.6)	49.5	(17.9)	50.5	(81.1)

Conclusions

In 1994 the highest risk of poverty for all three poverty lines was for villages and towns with a population of less than 3,000. For the income lines the lowest rate was observed in Dublin but for the combined income and deprivation line the poverty rate was a good deal lower in open country areas than in any other location. While the extent of change between 1987 and 1994 varied across poverty lines, a general trend towards a narrowing of differentials across areas was observed, as a consequence of an erosion of the advantage which Dublin had enjoyed at an earlier date.

In relation to incidence, for each poverty line the percentage of poor households in open country areas declined substantially. This was balanced by corresponding increases in the proportions accounted for by Dublin households. Both of these types of households have come over time to contain a proportion of the poor closer to what we would expect on the basis of the overall number of households they represent. In the case of the combined income and deprivation line the open country areas contained significantly less households than we would have expected on the basis of population.

Local authority renters experienced a rapid increase in poverty risks. By 1994 one half were below the 50 per cent income line, three quarters below the 60 per cent income line and one in two below the combined income and deprivation line. Despite the fact that overall the combined income and deprivation poverty rate fell over time, the risk for those in local authority housing rose. The declining number of public sector residents, however, ensured that poverty did not become more concentrated in local authority housing.

When we consider the combined income and deprivation line we find that while as in 1987 those in local authority housing in villages and towns with populations of less than 3,000 had the highest poverty rates, by 1994 they were now much more similar to other local authority tenants; with the exception of those in open country areas. This increased homogeneity was attributable to significant increases in poverty rates among local authority households in larger areas but particularly in Dublin. Declining or static rates of poverty in these areas led to wider differentials between the public and private sector. This disparity is significantly greater in the main urban centres. By 1994 two out of three local authority renters in Dublin were below the combined income and deprivation threshold; while in other urban centres the figure was in excess of one out of two.

Over time poverty has not become concentrated in local authority housing. It has, however, become more concentrated in public sector housing in Dublin where over 1 in 5 poor households are now found. Urban local authority households now account for three out of ten poor households. However, the problem of poverty clearly extends beyond the stereotypical urban poor.

Chapter 5

Understanding Variation in Poverty by Area and Tenure Type

Introduction

In addition to documenting variation in poverty rates by location and tenure we also seek to establish the extent to which such variation is causal in nature. To what extent could the patterns we observe arise solely because poverty and tenure and location are jointly associated with other factors which are the true determinants of poverty?

The Role of Unemployment and Social Class

In attempting to address this question a useful first step is to examine the pattern of unemployment and social class composition by area and tenure type. At this stage we focus on unemployment of the household head, and on whether the head is a member of the unskilled manual working class according to the Central Statistics Office's social class categorisation. The overall risk of unemployment for household heads was just under 11 per cent in both the 1994 and 1987 surveys.[1] Table 5.1 shows the unemployment rate for household heads by area type, from which we can see there was very little change between 1987 and 1994. The highest risk of unemployment at both points in time is found in villages and small towns, and the lowest levels in open country areas and Dublin. The percentage of household heads in unskilled manual work was also stable over time at about 15 per cent. The table shows that once again there was very little change between 1987 and 1994 in the pattern by area type. At both points in time the highest proportion in unskilled manual work

---

[1] Note that the overall unemployment rate in the 1994 survey was lower than in 1987, consistent with the decline of two percentage points in the unemployment rate over that period shown by the CSO's Labour Force Survey.

is in villages and towns with populations of less than 3,000, and the lowest proportion in that class are in Dublin.

Table 5.1: Risk of Household Head Being Unemployed/ Unskilled Manual Work by Type of Area 1987 and 1994

	Percentage of Unemployed Heads of Households by Type of Area		Percentage of Unskilled Manual Heads of Households by Type of Area	
	1987	1994	1987	1994
	Per Cent			
Open Country	6.5	7.3	15.6	16.3
Village/Town: <3,000	21.1	17.9	21.6	22.4
Town >3,000	12.7	13.3	15.2	15.7
Waterford, Cork, Galway and Limerick cities	18.5	15.3	16.8	15.1
Dublin city and county	8.8	8.4	10.9	11.8
All	10.9	10.6	15.1	15.4

Taking an incidence perspective, the results presented in Table 5.2 again show little change between 1987 and 1994, and thus no tendency for unemployment or membership of the unskilled manual class to become more concentrated over time in any of the type of areas distinguished in this analysis. The variation in unemployment rates across areas produces a situation where unemployed heads of households are distributed across type of area much more evenly than the population as a whole. While over 60 per cent of households are located in either Dublin or open country, the relatively low unemployment rates for household heads in these areas mean that they contain only 46 per cent of households with an unemployed head. The distribution of unskilled manual workers looks very much like the overall distribution of households, except that a smaller proportion are located in Dublin city and county and a slightly higher proportion in villages and towns with populations below 3,000.

Table 5.2: Percentage of Unemployed Heads of Households and Unskilled Manual Working Class Located in Each Type of Area for 1987 and 1994

	Percentage of Unemployed Heads of Households		Percentage of Unskilled Manual Heads of Households	
	1987	1994	1987	1994
	Per Cent			
Open Country	21.3	22.9	37.1	35.4
Village/Town: <3,000	21.8	17.8	16.1	14.3
Town >3,000	21.0	23.0	18.2	19.0
Waterford, Cork, Galway, Limerick cities	14.7	12.6	9.6	8.2
Dublin city and county	21.2	23.6	19.0	23.1
All	100.0	100.0	100.0	100.0

In Table 5.3 we again look at the proportion of household heads unemployed and the proportion in unskilled manual work, this time by housing tenure. In relation to unemployment, the picture is once more very much one of no change over time. The highest unemployment rate is found, not surprisingly, among local authority tenants, where one in three household heads are unemployed. Next come local authority tenant purchasers and private rental households, for whom about 16 per cent are unemployed. Finally, the unemployment rate for household heads in owner-occupied households (whether with a mortgage or not) is as low as 6 per cent.

For the percentage of heads in unskilled manual work, the rank ordering of tenure categories in 1994 is somewhat different. Local authority tenants are once again the most disadvantaged, with over one third falling into this lowest class category. They are now followed more closely by local authority tenant purchasers, for whom 25 per cent of heads are in the unskilled working class. Private tenants and those owning outright are grouped together with approximately 15 per cent of household heads at the bottom of the class hierarchy. Finally, mortgage holders display a distinctively low level, with only 5 per cent of heads found in the unskilled manual class. Between 1987 and 1994, the table shows that for households in local authority rented accommodation, there has been a significant increase in the proportion headed by someone in the unskilled manual class.

Table 5.3: Risk of Household Head Being Unemployed/ in Unskilled Manual Work by Tenure Type[2]

	Percentage of Unemployed Heads of Household by Tenure Type		Percentage of Unskilled Manual Heads of Household by Tenure Type	
	1987	1994	1987	1994
	Per cent			
Owned Outright	5.7	5.8	14.9	16.4
Owned with Mortgage	5.8	5.8	4.8	5.0
Local Authority Tenant Purchase	12.5	17.4	26.7	24.5
Local Authority Rented	33.6	33.5	29.8	37.3
Private Rented	16.5	15.8	12.6	14.0
All	10.9	10.6	15.0	15.2

Table 5.4 shows the distribution of household heads in unemployment and in unskilled manual work by tenure type. We see that 45 per cent of households with an unemployed head were in local authority rented housing in 1987 but by 1994 this had fallen to 37 per cent, because the proportion of all households in this tenure type declined while their unemployment rate remained constant. There have been corresponding increases in the proportion of unemployed heads who are in the owner-occupied with mortgage, local authority tenant-purchase, and, in particular, private tenant categories. The distribution of households in the unskilled manual class has also changed somewhat, with the proportion in local authority housing falling and the proportion in the private rented sector and owner-occupied with mortgage increasing. By 1994, little more than one in four unskilled manual households are in local authority rented housing, and only 38 per cent in all are in public sector housing, either rental or tenant-purchase.

---

[2] The unemployment rates quoted here are for household heads. The rate for all individuals are in line with the Labour Force Survey estimates (see Callan et al., 1996: 46–47).

Table 5.4: Percentage Unemployed Household Heads and Unskilled Working Class Found in Each Type of Tenure

	Percentage of Unemployed Heads of Household		Percentage of Unskilled Heads of Household	
	1987	1994	1987	1994
	Per cent			
Owned Outright	23.7	23.0	44.1	44.4
Owned with Mortgage	15.1	17.6	9.0	11.3
Local Authority Tenant Purchase	8.9	10.4	13.7	10.8
Local Authority Rented	44.9	37.0	28.9	27.3
Private Rented	7.9	12.0	4.4	7.2
All	100.0	100.0	100.0	100.0

The worsening risk of being in the unskilled manual class for local authority tenants and of unemployment for tenant-purchasers may be, at least in part, a consequence of housing policy over the period. The decline in the overall proportion of households in local authority housing between 1987 and 1994 in the two surveys is consistent with the falling supply of local authority housing. Fahey and Watson (1995) note that during the years from 1987 to 1992 the local authority house building programme slowed to one-quarter of the average over the previous twenty years. That decline, they note, was prompted by falling numbers but also by the continuing high rate of sales of local authority housing to tenants. Sales numbered over 18,000 houses in 1989, the highest annual total on record, and totalled over 31,000 houses in the years 1989–1991. The combination of the decline in the building programme and high sales sharply depleted the total local authority housing stock.

Fahey and Watson note that a tension exists between the two principal objectives of Irish housing policy — the promotion of home ownership and the provision of an adequate standard of housing. The tenant purchase scheme, they observe, had the potential to increase social stability and reduce residualisation by encouraging higher income tenants to remain in the local authority estates, but such an outcome was dependent on the extent to which such purchases have contributed to a mix of tenures and social circumstances *within* estates rather than to distinctions along these lines *between* such estates:

> "Certainly in the larger cities there has been a tendency for the bulk of the housing in some estates to be purchased over time by the tenants while other estates — typically in the less desirable areas remain in local authority tenure. When this happens the social housing sector becomes residualised — a residual of those who lack the means to become owner occupiers and a residual of housing when many of the more desirable houses have been bought — so that some local authority housing has a strong association with lone parenthood, unemployment, poverty, area segregation and other forms of marginalisation." (Fahey and Watson, 1995: 22)

The evidence we have presented of an increased risk of poverty for local authority tenants between 1987 and 1994 is consistent with such a process of residualisation, but a more definitive statement on this issue must await our consideration of the manner in which housing tenure effects are mediated by other influences. Our findings relating to the increased level of poverty among local authority purchasers is also consistent with Fahey and Watson's argument that the promotion of home ownership may not only have the consequence of "creaming off" the top tier of housing applicants, but may not be in the best interests of some of the purchasers. Some of these families may run into difficulties if confronted with a long-term inflexible pattern of payments at a period in the life-cycle when expenses are rising. Another feature of housing-related policy over the period is the increasing role of rent and mortgage supplements through the Supplementary Welfare Allowance scheme, where expenditure increased sevenfold between 1989 and 1994 (Fahey and Watson, 1995: 166). It is interesting in that context that our survey evidence shows an increase in the proportion of poor households who are either owner-occupiers with a mortgage or in private rented accommodation between 1987 and 1994 — reflecting the increase in the importance of these tenure types in the population as a whole, rather than an increase in their poverty risk relative to other tenure types.

Conclusions

In both 1987 and 1994 the lowest risk of unemployment for the head of household was observed in the least and most densely populated locations. Elsewhere relatively modest variation was observed. This pattern of risk leads to a situation where the unemployed are more evenly spread across our area categories than are the population as a whole. The likelihood that the head of household is in the unskilled manual working class is spread more evenly across areas with Dublin once again displaying the lowest rates. As a consequence, at both points in time, seven out of ten households found in this class were located outside the main urban centres and over one in three were in open country areas.

Once again there is little evidence of geographical concentration and it is tenure which proves to be the more potent explanatory factor. One in three local authority renters have a head of household in the unskilled manual class: a rate which is twice that of any other type of tenure. The only suggestion of significant change over time concerns the deteriorating position of local authority tenant purchasers. A similar pattern of risk is evident for unemployment with the exception of the fact that the disparity between types of local authority households is much less. In 1987 their level of risk was almost equal but by 1994 there had been a significant increase in the probability of local authority tenants being drawn from the unskilled working class.

Over time unemployment of heads of households became less concentrated in local authority housing. There has also been an increase in the proportion of the unskilled manual class being found in the private sector. This pattern is consistent with changes in housing policy which may have disproportionately self selected the skilled section of the working class out of local authority rented housing while at the same time making it more difficult for unskilled manual workers to enter such housing. Thus, at the same time as public sector rented housing becomes more homogenous in class terms, more recent entrants to other segments of the housing market are likely to have higher rates of unemployment than their predecessors.

Chapter 6

Assessing the Net Effect of Location and Tenure

Introduction

The fact that a specific type of area or tenure has a relatively high poverty rate does not in itself indicate anything about the impact of location or tenure *per se* on poverty: it could be entirely attributable to the socio-economic composition of the households involved. Households renting local authority housing could be at high risk of poverty, for example, because — as Fahey and Watson (1995) note — applicants tend to be drawn from the most vulnerable sectors of the population: the unemployed, lone parents, the elderly and those unable to work. Cross-tabulations can only take one so far in understanding variation in poverty risk by area/tenure type at a point in time or the changes in this pattern observed between 1987 and 1994. We therefore now systematically examine the extent to which the observed variation in risk of poverty by area and housing tenure effects may be attributable to differences in the measured characteristics of those located in different areas or in different types of tenure, using logistic regressions.[1] This procedure allows one to assess the effect of any particular factor on the odds of being poor while holding constant the influence of other factors.

---

[1] It might appear more straightforward to define a dependent dummy variable where being poor is scored 1 and non-poor 0 and proceed to use ordinary least squares regression in order to predict the probability of being poor. However, there are two difficulties with such an approach. First, predicted values can lie outside the range of 0 to 1. Second, the variability of the residuals will depend on the size of the independent variable. This condition, known as *heteroscedasticity*, implies that the estimates for the regression coefficient, although unbiased (not systematically too high or low) will not be efficient in the sense of having a small standard. For accessible treatments of logistic regression see Menard (1995) and Liao (1994).

Methodology

The notion of odds is one very familiar to all gamblers. Suppose 20 per cent of the population are poor. Instead of saying that the probability of being poor is 0.2 and of not being poor is 0.8, we can say that the odds on being poor is 0.25 (ie. 0.2/0.8) and the odds on being non-poor is 4:1 (0.8/0.2). An actual example taken from Table 4.3 will help to further illustrate the relationship between the risk of poverty and odds ratios. In 1994, 5.5 per cent of mortgage holders fell below the combined 60 per cent mean income and basic deprivation line — giving them a 0.058 (5.5/94.5) chance of being poor. On the other hand, fifty-two per cent of local authority tenants fell below this line, so for them the corresponding odds were 1.08 (52/48). The disparity between the two groups can be indexed by the ratio of these odds (1.08/0.058), which gives us an odds ratio of 18.6 to 1. In other words, the odds on public sector tenants being poor are 18.6 times higher than the odds for mortgage holders. By choosing any group as a reference point we can summarise the set of inequalities between that group and all others. This also allows one to derive the odds ratio between any two of the other groups being employed. From Table 4.3 we also see that 24.5 per cent of local authority purchasers were poor, so their odds ratio *vis-à-vis* mortgage holders is 5.6. Thus, given that the odds ratio between local authority tenants and mortgage holders is 18.6, and the odds ratio between local authority purchasers and mortgage holders is 5.6, then by implication the odds ratio between local authority tenants and local authority purchasers is 3.3 (18.6/5.6). It is more convenient to work with odds because the predicted impact of a change in any factor on the probability of being poor from an estimated logistic regression depends on the values of other independent variables. This is because it is harder to bring about a change in the probability of a particular outcome if the value is at the extremes of the distribution. Thus the change in the value of any factor has less impact on the probability of being poor for households who previously had particularly high or low risks of poverty than for those experiencing moderate risk.[2]

The analysis proceeds as follows. First, we will present the odds ratios for being poor rather than non-poor by type of housing tenure. (We combine the categories of outright ownership and mortgage holders in the results presented since differences between these groups

---

[2] It is important, however, to keep clearly in mind, as Menard (1995: 13) stresses "that the probability, the odds and the logit are three different ways of expressing exactly the same thing".

disappear once we control for socio-demographic factors.) Then we examine the interaction between tenure and location in an urban centre which our earlier analysis has shown to be of particular significance. Finally, and most importantly, we examine the consequences for the estimated area type and tenure effects and their interaction when controlling for a range of other social influences. When implementing such a procedure it is impossible to be sure that we have controlled for all relevant factors. However, the information available to us from the 1987 and 1994 surveys allows us to control for a particularly comprehensive set of variables. Because of the evidence from our earlier analysis of the particularly high poverty rates experienced by local authority tenants in Dublin, we then repeat this analysis distinguishing between Dublin and elsewhere rather than between urban and rural areas. We continue to focus on the combined 60 per cent of mean income and basic deprivation poverty standard.

Housing Tenure

In Table 6.1 we show, for both 1987 and 1994, the odds ratios of being poor rather than non-poor with these figures being calculated from estimated logistic regressions using owner-occupiers (both outright owners and mortgage holders) as the reference category.[3] In 1987 the odds on a household renting a local authority dwelling being poor was 7.2 times that of this reference group. By 1994 the relative situation of public sector tenants had deteriorated, to such an extent that this odds ratio reached almost 12. Local authority purchasers also experienced a worsening in their relative situation as the odds ratio more than doubled, from 1.5 to 3.6. The situation of private tenants deteriorated from almost unity to a value of two. Overall, then, disparities in poverty risks between outright owners and mortgage holders and all other types of tenure widened between 1987 and 1994. At the same time there was a slight narrowing of the gap between renters and purchasers in the public sector.

---

[3] The equations employed allowed all possible interactions between tenure and urban-rural location.

Table 6.1: Ratios of Being Poor versus Non-Poor for the Combined 60% Income and Basic Deprivation Measure by Type of Tenure

	Odds Ratio	
	1987	*1994*
Outright Owners and Mortgage Holders	1.00	1.00
Private Tenants	1.01	1.99
Local Authority Purchasers	1.54	3.55
Local Authority Tenants	7.21	11.73

Housing Tenure and Urban-Rural Location

In Table 6.2 we set out the odds ratios arising from the combination of housing tenure and urban-rural location.[4] In 1987, the odds on public sector renters in both urban and rural areas being poor were more than seventeen times higher than that of urban owner-occupiers. Private tenants in urban areas had somewhat higher ratios than their rural counterparts. On the other hand rural local authority purchasers had higher ratios than those in urban areas — 4.87 compared to 2.89. By 1994 some dramatic changes could be observed. In urban centres, the disparity in odds of being poor between local authority renters and owner-occupiers had almost doubled and the odds ratio now stood at over 30:1. Outside the urban centres the corresponding ratio actually fell to 13:1. Thus, from a position close to equality in 1987, the odds on being poor for public sector tenants in urban centres were substantially higher than for their rural counterparts by 1994. Overall, the situation of those in public sector housing, whether rental or tenant-purchase, deteriorated in comparison with other groups. However, the most significant change is the widening of the gap between local authority tenants in urban centres and other groups.

---

[4] Urban refers to the main urban centres Dublin, Cork, Limerick, Galway and Waterford.

Table 6.2: Odds Ratios of Being Poor versus Non-Poor by Type of Housing Tenure and Urban-Rural Location

	1987		1994	
	Urban	Rural	Urban	Rural
Outright Owners and Mortgage Holders	1.00	3.19	1.00	2.09
Private Tenants	3.09	1.77	2.62	3.85
Local Authority Purchasers	2.89	4.87	4.85	8.04
Local Authority Tenants	17.31	18.33	30.55	13.02

The results presented in Table 6.2 are the outcome of a number of effects:

- Type of tenure is strongly related to risk of poverty. Local authority tenants suffer by far the highest degree of exposure to poverty. They are followed by local authority purchasers and by private renters. By far the lowest level is observed among outright owners and mortgage holders.

- There is an overall tendency for poverty rates to be lower in urban centres.

- However, this is counteracted by the fact that tenure effects are stronger in urban centres than elsewhere. This effect is strongest for local authority tenants but is also evident for local authority purchasers and private tenants.

- The overall impact of urban-rural location declined across time while the consequences of tenure increased.

- Finally, the trend towards an increased impact for local authority tenancy to increase the risk of poverty was greatest in urban centres.

Socio-Demographic Influence in Urban and Rural Locations

We wish to establish, as far as possible, the extent to which these effects and their trends over time can be accounted for by the socio-demographic characteristics of the households in different areas and tenure types. In Table 6.3, therefore, we present the same set of odds ratios as in Table 6.2, but now the estimated logistic regression equations from which they are calculated include as additional independent variables characteristics of the head of household such as social class, education, labour force status, marital status, childhood economic circumstances, whether there is a partner in the household, if the partner is in full-time work and number of children. Looking first at 1987, we see that, for both urban and rural households, the disparity between public sector renters and urban owner-occupiers is reduced from 17–18:1 to about 5:1. Approximately three quarters of the original estimated effect of being a local authority tenant on poverty risk is thus accounted for by our control variables. The introduction of socio-demographic characteristics also substantially reduces the impact of being a local authority tenant-purchaser and somewhat more modestly the effect of being a private tenant and a rural owner or mortgage holder.

Table 6.3: Odds Ratios of Being Poor versus Non-Poor by Type of Housing Tenure and Urban-Rural Location Controlling for Socio-Demographic Influence

| | 1987 | | 1994 | |
	Urban	*Rural*	*Urban*	*Rural*
Outright Owners and Mortgage Holders	1.00	2.60	1.00	1.50
Private Tenants	2.07	1.14	1.22	2.89
Local Authority Purchasers	1.61	2.03	1.53	2.10
Local Authority Tenants	5.09	5.32	6.07	2.13

Turning to the results for 1994, the comparison between Tables 6.2 and 6.3 shows that for urban households, the disparity between public sector renters and urban owner-occupiers is now reduced from over 30:1 to 6:1. Eighty per cent of the original estimated effect of being an urban local authority tenant on poverty risk is thus accounted for by our control variables. A slightly larger reduction is achieved for their rural counterparts for whom the residual odds ratio declines to 2:1. The increasing disadvantage experienced by local authority tenants over time is almost entirely accounted for, as indicated by the similarity of the residual odds ratios across time, by the socio-demographic characteristics of the households. However, the decline in the corresponding rural ratio suggests that there are other factors at play. The largest odds ratio in rural areas is now associated with private tenants, but tenure actually has little residual effect. Overall, the socio-demographic characteristics of households are seen to account for most of the variation in poverty rates across tenure and area types, and most of the changes in these differentials between 1987 and 1994. However, urban local authority renters do face a considerably higher probability of being in poverty than other tenure/area groups, even after controlling for the range of characteristics included as controls.

The odds ratio of 6:1 for that group in comparison with urban owner-occupiers provides an estimate of the maximum impact of factors associated with being in the urban local authority rental sector *per se*, which may require other types of explanation. It is a maximum because we cannot be sure that we have controlled for all of the influences which might mediate the influence of location. Attributing a residual effect to any particular variable inevitably exposes one to the danger that the subsequent inclusion of further control variables could reduce the remaining effects even further. We shall return to the question of what such factors might be in our conclusion.

Housing Tenure in Dublin versus Elsewhere

Given the particularly high poverty rates found earlier for local authority renters in Dublin, we now repeat this analysis distinguishing between Dublin and elsewhere rather than between urban and rural areas. Table 6.4 takes owner-occupiers in Dublin as the reference group, and shows the odds of being poor relative to that group by type of tenure and location in or outside Dublin, in the absence of any control variables. In 1987, the odds on local authority renters, both in and outside Dublin, being poor were about 25 times greater than for Dublin owner-occupiers. By 1994 a dramatic change was observed: the figure for local authority renters in Dublin rose to 35, while for those outside Dublin it fell to 15. The gap between public sector renters and owner-occupiers was now 4½ times greater in Dublin than elsewhere. The relative situation of owner-occupiers and private renters in rural areas improved over the period, while the situation of local authority tenant purchasers in Dublin got worse, but the dominant feature is the deteriorating position of public sector renters in Dublin.

Table 6.4: Odds on Being Poor versus Non-Poor by Type of Tenure, Dublin versus Elsewhere

| | 1987 | | 1994 | |
	Dublin	*Elsewhere*	*Dublin*	*Elsewhere*
Outright Owners and Mortgage Holders	1.00	4.43	1.00	1.98
Private Tenants	2.59	4.30	2.19	3.83
Local Authority Purchasers	4.52	6.37	5.84	6.17
Local Authority Tenants	24.37	26.04	35.47	15.53

Socio-Economic Influence in Dublin and Elsewhere

In Table 6.5 we repeat the procedure of introducing the set of control variables. Comparison with Table 6.4 shows that in 1987 these variables account for 70 per cent of the disparity between public sector renters and owner-occupiers in Dublin, and 75 per cent of the gap between the latter group and local authority tenants outside Dublin. The residual odds ratio for Dublin local authority renters was about 7.7:1, and for those outside Dublin it was about 6.7:1. None of the other odds ratios goes significantly above 3:1. Turning to 1994, the introduction of the control variables accounts for 80 per cent of the gap between owner-occupiers in Dublin and local authority renters, whether in Dublin or outside. The striking gap which remains, despite these controls, is between local authority renters versus home-owners in Dublin, where the odds ratio is 7:1. However, this figure is marginally lower than the corresponding figure for 1987, which was 7.7:1, so the socio-demographic control variables entirely explain most of the deterioration in the position of this group over time. They are less successful, however, in explaining the improved position of local authority tenants outside Dublin. The disparities for other groups which remain in 1994 when the controls are included are rather modest, with the largest odds ratio being little greater than two.

Table 6.5: Odds on Being Poor versus Non-Poor by Type of Housing Tenure, Dublin versus Elsewhere Controlling for Socio-Demographic Variables

| | 1987 | | 1994 | |
	Dublin	Elsewhere	Dublin	Elsewhere
Outright Owners and Mortgage Holders	1.00	3.24	1.00	1.50
Private Tenants	2.00	2.10	1.95	2.89
Local Authority Purchasers	3.28	2.57	1.83	2.10
Local Authority Tenants	7.72	6.66	6.89	2.13

Conclusions

In this chapter we set out to test the extent to which the impact of type of tenure on risk of poverty could be accounted for by other factors. It is worth noting that the set of variables which we introduce as controls is a fairly parsimonious one. It comprises the social class, education, childhood circumstances, labour force status and labour market experience of the household head and a small number of variables relating to household structure. The basic fact which requires explanation is that local authority tenancy, local authority purchase and private tenancy are associated, in that order of magnitude, with increased risks of poverty. These effects are particularly evident in urban centres. Furthermore the impact of housing tenure increased between 1987 and 1994. In general, the set of control variables we employ do rather a good job of explaining tenure effects. In particular, in 1994, eighty per cent of the effect of being a local authority tenant was accounted for by other characteristics of the household. In addition, the increased risk of poverty suffered by local authority households in urban centres was shown to be a consequence of these mediating variables. On the other hand, the decline in risk of poverty for rural local authority households was not entirely accounted for by our control variables. When we compare Dublin with the rest of the country, we observe particularly high levels of risk for Dublin local authority tenants but the manner in which these effects are mediated, and the pattern of change, is broadly similar to that already described for urban centres; both Dublin and other urban centres have changed in relation to rural locations in a very similar fashion.

When we say that changes in tenure effects over time are accounted for by our control variables what we wish to communicate is
that increased risk of poverty is a consequence either of the impact of
particular variables or/and a changing pattern of differences between
types of tenure on some of the control variables. A full explanation of
these changes would require a comprehensive analysis of patterns of
cumulative disadvantage and the manner in which they have
changed over time. Such an analysis forms part of our ongoing research agenda. Our analysis to date suggests that an understanding
of changing tenure effects requires that we take into account the
changing impact of factors such as urban-rural location, farming, unemployment and education, and the changing disparities between
types of household tenure in terms of absence of a partner to the head
of household, levels of education and incidence of long-term unemployment.

Having introduced our set of mediating variables we still find per-
sisting tenure effects, in particular, the odds of urban local authority
tenants being poor are six times greater than those for urban house
owners and mortgage holders. As we have indicated, this provides an
estimate of the maximum extent of the impact of being a local
authority tenant household which requires explanation in terms
other than the socio-demographic characteristics of such households.
However, there are considerable difficulties in interpreting this
residual odds-ratio. A comparable example is that of attributing
gender differentials in earnings, which cannot be explained by measured socio-demographic characteristics, to discrimination. We cannot
be certain that there are not other relevant differences between the
two types of households. In the present case we are inclined to be
particularly cautious because our analysis to date has allowed type of
tenure to interact solely with location. This path was chosen because
it was precisely such interactions which were central to the questions
which we wished to address. However, we cannot rule out the possibility that the impact of local authority tenancy may vary in relation
to other characteristics such as employment status of the household
or the presence or absence of a partner. The nature of such interactions is likely to provide support for alternative explanations of tenure effects. In any event, an attempt to further account for tenure
effects through associated household characteristics must explore
such interactions or introduce additional control variables which,
while associated with risk of poverty, are largely unrelated to the set
which we have included in our analysis. On the other hand those who
wish to argue the case for locational and/or tenure effects, which are

not reducible to socio-demographic characteristics of households need to find ways of establishing such effects, other than as residual elements in household models.

Chapter 7

Risk of Poverty by Planning Region

Introduction

Up to this point our spatial analysis has actually been based on a mixture of type of location and actual areas. Such an analysis does not generate a mapping of poverty rates. The extent to which such a mapping can be achieved with the survey data available to us is limited. As pointed out earlier, sample size in the 1987 and 1994 surveys does not allow a reliable disaggregation of poverty rates or incidence to county level or below. However, it is possible to look at a higher level of aggregation, namely the planning regions which group counties as follows:

East: Dublin, Kildare, Meath, Wicklow;
South-West: Cork, Kerry;
South-East: Carlow, Kilkenny, South Tipperary, Waterford,
               Wexford;
North-East: Cavan, Louth, Monaghan;
Mid-West: Clare, Limerick, North Tipperary;
Midlands: Laois, Longford, Offaly, Roscommon, Westmeath;
West: Galway, Mayo;
North-West: Leitrim, Sligo;
Donegal: Donegal.

If we combine Donegal with the North-West, there are sufficient numbers in each sample in each of the eight different regions to permit analysis, though the results must be treated with caution.[1]

---

[1] In the 1987 Survey there were at least 200 households in each of these regions while in the 1994 Survey there were at least 300.

Risk of Poverty by Planning Region

Table 7.1 shows the risk of poverty for the 50 per cent and 60 per cent income lines and the combined 60 per cent income and basic deprivation standard by region for 1987 and 1994. In 1987 across all three poverty lines the risk of poverty was lowest in the East and highest in the North-West and Donegal. Variation between the other areas was relatively modest, although the North-East had relatively high rates and the West comparatively low ones. The results for 1994 show some substantial shifts. With the income poverty lines, the most marked is the increase in poverty rates in the East region. With the combined income and deprivation standard, the rate for the East remains stable but that for a number of other regions falls substantially — notably for the North-East, Mid-West, Midlands and West. As a result, although the East continues to have the lowest poverty rates at both income lines in 1994, the differences between it and the other regions are now quite modest. With the combined income/deprivation standard, by 1994 there are several regions with lower rates than the East, notably the West. The North-West and Donegal continue to display the highest poverty rate for the 50 and 60 per cent income lines and for the combined income and deprivation standard.

Table 7.1: Risk of Poverty by Planning Region 1987 and 1994

	50% Income Line Risk		60% Income Line Risk		60% Line + Deprivation Risk	
	1987	1994	1987	1994	1987	1994
	Per Cent					
East	9.6	16.0	19.3	29.1	13.6	13.6
South-West	17.7	17.9	31.0	34.4	16.3	13.0
South-East	20.8	23.0	33.3	40.0	16.9	18.3
North-East	24.6	15.9	35.7	38.2	20.6	12.8
Mid-West	20.5	22.0	32.9	39.2	19.7	13.4
Midlands	21.7	21.4	41.1	39.7	19.7	13.1
West	19.6	20.2	31.0	35.5	13.8	7.3
North West and Donegal	27.3	24.7	42.6	43.5	22.9	23.5
Total	16.9	18.9	29.0	34.7	16.4	14.9

For both income lines there has been a considerable narrowing in differential poverty risks over time, but this has not happened with the combined income/deprivation standard. Consistent with our earlier analysis, the overall impression which emerges is of the modest scale of variation by area in poverty risks.

Incidence of Poverty by Planning Region

In Table 7.2 we look at spatial variation in the incidence rather than risk of poverty by region. Changes in incidence between 1987 and 1994 are a product of the changes in risk pattern just described, and the changing distribution of all households over the regions which is also shown in Table 7.2. Across the three poverty standards, the proportion of all poor households located in the North-East, the Mid-West, and the West declined over the period, while the proportion in the East increased. By 1994, the distribution of poor households is particularly close to the overall distribution of households by region using the combined income and deprivation standard. With the income poverty lines, the East region still has a smaller share of the poor than of the population, though this is less pronounced than in 1987.

Table 7.2: Incidence of Poverty by Planning Region in 1987 and 1994

	50% Income Line Incidence		60% Income Line Incidence		60% Income Line + Basic Deprivation Incidence		Percentage of Households	
	1987	1994	1987	1994	1987	1994	1987	1994
	Per cent							
East	20.2	32.2	23.7	31.9	29.5	39.9	35.6	38.1
South-West	16.1	14.8	16.5	15.4	15.3	13.7	15.4	15.5
South-East	11.0	12.7	10.2	12.0	9.2	13.0	8.9	10.4
North-East	8.6	4.5	7.3	5.9	7.4	4.7	5.9	5.4
Mid-West	13.2	10.2	12.4	9.9	13.0	7.8	10.9	8.9
Midlands	8.6	8.3	9.5	8.4	7.9	6.3	6.7	7.3
West	11.0	7.9	10.2	7.6	8.0	3.6	9.5	7.4
North-West and Donegal	11.3	9.2	10.3	8.8	9.8	11.0	9.0	6.9
Total	100.0	100.0	100.0	100.0	100.0	100.0	100.0	100.0

Conclusions

In 1987, for the 50 per cent and 60 per cent income lines, the most significant aspect of spatial variation was the distinctively low risk levels observed for the East. The significant increase in poverty rates observed for this area results in a spatial distribution of risk which is much more homogenous by 1994. The level of poverty remains highest for the North-West and Donegal and lowest for Dublin. Variation by location for the combined income and deprivation line was a good deal more modest in 1987. By 1994, if one leaves aside a particularly high rate in the North-West and Donegal and a correspondingly low one in the West, there is remarkably little variation by region. By 1994 the distribution of poor households based on the combined poverty and deprivation measure comes near to reproducing the overall distribution of households. The processes which produce poverty appear to operate with equal strength across the kind of spatial divisions captured in the planning regions schema.

Chapter 8

Spatial Variations in Poverty Surrogates Using Evidence from the Census

Introduction

Up to this point we have considered variations in poverty risk and incidence using household survey data. If we are to consider spatial variations in poverty below the regional level of aggregation, we must turn to another data source, namely the Small Area Population Statistics (SAPS) derived from the Census of Population. These constitute the most geographically disaggregated and comprehensive information on the socio-demographic structure of the country, with the most recently available data relating to 1991. The variables available from the census include the structure of the population according to age; sex; labour force status; levels of educational attainment; age at which full-time education was completed; social class; socio-economic group; family type; status of tenure; provision of sanitary facilities and age of the housing stock. The slightly unwieldy label of "surrogates of poverty" is necessary to draw attention to the fact that no information on income is collected in the census, so it is not possible to use the SAPS to directly derive estimates of the risk or incidence of income poverty in an area. Nor do we have an adequate sample of indicators which would allow us to construct a measure such as the basic deprivation dimension employed in our survey analysis. What one can do, however, is to use the census data to examine spatial variations in the prevalence of characteristics which are known to be strongly correlated with poverty. However, precisely because of the absence of an adequate measure for the dependent variable, we are not in a position to establish how well any such socio-demographic characteristic succeeds in predicting poverty or deprivation.

The most disaggregated unit of analysis available from the SAPS data is the District Electoral Division (DED) of which there is a total of just over 3,400 throughout the country as a whole. The DEDs can be aggregated in any way to provide details on the sub-national demographic structure at any level of aggregation. In the current chapter we use the Rural District level as the unit of aggregation for presenting the data in map form. These maps contain 159 areal units. There is, in fact, a total of 217 Rural and Urban Districts (RDs and UDs) in the country as a whole. For convenience and clarity of presentation we have incorporated the Urban Districts in their relevant Rural District as appropriate for mapping purposes.[1]

The reader should note two important points when interpreting the Small Area Population Statistics. First, the Census data do not provide information on households or persons *per se*, but rather on the socio-demographic characteristics of *areas*. The unit of analysis is the district electoral division, the rural district, the county, the planning region, etc., depending on the level of geographical aggregation under consideration in any given table.

Secondly, in undertaking any analysis or description of geographically-based or area data the results will, to some degree, be dependent on the scale of spatial units chosen. Geographical units are, in the main, neither immutable nor objectively defined. In theory, an infinity of geographical subdivisions could be devised for use in any analysis or description of regional data. Differences in the geographical unit chosen may result in (at least minor) differences in the results depending on the inclusion or exclusion of a set of individuals with any given set of characteristics. Thus, modifications to the geographical unit of analysis may give rise to slight differences in the results. This problem has been described in the geographical literature as the Modifiable Areal Unit Problem (MAUP). This problem has been found to substantially affect the interrelationships between variables. In general, it has been found that the higher the level of spatial aggregation (i.e. the smaller the number of areal units used in the analysis) the larger will be the correlation coefficients between the variables. The problem was first documented by Gehlke and Biehl (1934) when they observed that the correlation coefficient between male juvenile delinquency and median monthly income across 252 census tracts in Cleveland increased as the level of spatial aggregation increased to a maximum of 25 tracts. There is little that one can do about this modifiable areal unit problem (particularly in the context

---

[1] For convenience throughout the chapter we subsequently use the term Rural District to refer to the aggregated Rural/Urban district area. See Appendix at the end of the book for a reference outlining the 159 Rural Districts.

of the current report). It is important, however, that the reader is aware of the potential significance of the problem and interprets the data accordingly.[2]

In the remainder of this chapter we use the 1986 and 1991 SAPS data to examine spatial variations in variables which are known to be strongly related to poverty. We consider spatial variations in the risk and incidence of unemployment and discuss variations in the distribution of persons in the unskilled manual class category. Finally, we describe the distribution of private permanent household rentals from the local authority. Throughout the chapter we present a national picture at the county level in tabular form as well as in map form at the rural district level. In addition, a detailed description of the position within Dublin is presented at the level of the electoral ward.[3]

Unemployment

Perhaps the single most important proxy of poverty and disadvantage available from the SAPS is level of unemployment. A great deal of research undertaken into poverty and its correlates in Ireland has identified the importance of unemployment as a factor in the generation and perpetuation of poverty.[4] By examining spatial variations in unemployment we can substantially advance our understanding of the geography of poverty, deprivation and disadvantage.

Unemployment — the National Picture

Table 8.1 presents details on the variation in county unemployment rates for both 1986 and 1991 as well as the *incidence* of unemployment or distribution across the counties of persons who are unemployed in both years. The first four columns in the table relate to variations in the rate of unemployment by county. From this one can see that the national rate for 1986 was 17.9 per cent falling to 16.9 per cent by 1991. At the level of the county we can see that those with the highest rates in 1991 include Donegal; Limerick County Borough;

---

[2] For a concise discussion of the modifiable areal unit problem see Clark and Avery (1976); Oppenshaw and Taylor (1982); Oppenshaw (1984a; b) and Fotheringham and Wong (1991).

[3] There are a total of 322 wards in the Dublin City (County Borough) and county areas.

[4] See, for example, Rottman et al., (1982); Roche (1984); Callan et al., (1989); Whelan et al., (1991); Nolan and Callan (1994); Callan et al., (1996).

Louth; Dublin County Borough and Cork County Borough — all in the range 21–25 per cent. Counties with the lowest rates of unemployment in 1991 include Roscommon, Cork County, Cavan, Clare and Leitrim all with rates in the range of 10–14 per cent.[5] It is clear from the table that the general trends in the relativities of county-level unemployment rates in 1986 are consistent with those of 1991 and that, in general, the trend at the level of the individual county over the period in question reflects the national trend of one percentage point decline over the period in question.

---

[5] The reader's attention is drawn to the fact that counties such as Roscommon, Cavan, Clare and Leitrim have among the highest incidence of small-scale farming in the country. The under-employment associated with this scale of agricultural activity is not measured in the SAPS data, but may be deflating unemployment levels in the counties in question.

Table 8.1: Rates and Incidence of Unemployment by County, 1986 and 1991

| | Unemployment Rate | | | | Distribution of Persons | | | |
| | 1986 | | 1991 | | 1986 | | 1991 | |
	Per Cent	(Rank)	Per Cent	(Rank)	Unemployed	Aged 15+	Unemployed	Aged 15+
EAST REGION								
Dublin Co. Borough	21.7	(6)	21.7	(4)	20.0	15.6	19.8	14.8
Dublin County	15.0	(25)	14.1	(27)	12.4	14.0	13.4	15.1
Kildare	15.4	(21)	14.4	(23)	2.8	3.1	2.9	3.3
Meath	17.2	(15)	15.3	(17)	2.7	2.8	2.6	2.8
Wicklow	19.2	(8)	17.7	(10)	2.8	2.6	2.8	2.7
SOUTH-WEST REGION								
Cork Co. Borough	22.5	(4)	21.1	(5)	4.7	4.0	4.4	3.8
Cork County	14.4	(28)	12.5	(31)	6.1	7.7	5.8	7.9
Kerry	18.9	(9)	16.7	(12)	3.5	3.5	3.2	3.5
WEST REGION								
Galway Co. Borough	15.1	(24)	15.3	(16)	1.1	1.4	1.3	1.5
Galway County	15.5	(20)	15.2	(18)	3.1	3.7	3.2	3.6
Mayo	17.3	(14)	16.0	(14)	2.9	3.3	2.7	3.1
MIDLANDS REGION								
Laois	16.8	(16)	16.2	(13)	1.3	1.5	1.3	1.4
Longford	15.2	(23)	14.9	(21)	0.7	0.9	0.7	0.8
Offaly	18.9	(10)	17.1	(11)	1.7	1.6	1.6	1.6
Westmeath	14.8	(27)	14.3	(24)	1.4	1.8	1.4	1.7
Roscommon	11.7	(32)	10.2	(32)	1.0	1.6	0.8	1.5

Table 8.1: Rates and Incidence of Unemployment by County, 1986 and 1991

| | Unemployment Rate | | | | Distribution of Persons | | | |
| | 1986 | | 1991 | | 1986 | | 1991 | |
	Per Cent	(Rank)	Per Cent	(Rank)	Unemployed	Aged 15+	Unemployed	Aged 15+
SOUTH-EAST REGION								
Carlow	18.8	(12)	18.4	(8)	1.2	1.1	1.2	1.1
Kilkenny	15.9	(17)	15.1	(20)	1.8	2.0	1.8	2.1
Wexford	20.7	(7)	19.2	(7)	3.2	2.8	3.1	2.8
South Tipperary	18.8	(11)	18.1	(9)	2.2	2.1	2.2	2.1
Waterford Co. Borough	21.8	(5)	21.0	(6)	1.4	1.1	1.4	1.2
Waterford County	17.4	(13)	15.9	(15)	1.4	1.4	1.3	1.4
NORTH-EAST REGION								
Louth	22.7	(3)	22.2	(3)	3.3	2.5	3.3	2.5
Cavan	13.7	(30)	12.6	(30)	1.1	1.5	1.1	1.5
Monaghan	15.0	(26)	14.2	(26)	1.2	1.4	1.2	1.4
NORTH-WEST REGION								
Leitrim	14.3	(29)	13.7	(28)	0.6	0.8	0.5	0.7
Sligo	15.9	(18)	14.8	(22)	1.4	1.6	1.3	1.6
Donegal	27.1	(1)	25.4	(1)	5.1	3.6	5.1	3.5
MID-WEST REGION								
Clare	13.2	(31)	13.3	(29)	1.9	2.5	2.0	2.6
Limerick Co. Borough	25.1	(2)	25.3	(2)	2.3	1.6	2.2	1.5
Limerick County	15.3	(22)	14.2	(25)	2.6	3.0	2.6	3.1
North Tipperary	15.8	(19)	15.1	(19)	1.4	1.7	1.4	1.6
State	17.9		16.9		100	100	100	100

Rural/Urban district unemployment rates are presented in Maps 8.1 and 8.2 for 1986 and 1991 respectively. One can see from the former map that, in general, districts with the highest levels of unemployment in 1991 were found in parts of counties Donegal, north and west Mayo into parts of west Galway; north and south-west Kerry and in a long tract through parts of counties Wicklow, Wexford, Waterford, Kilkenny, Kildare and Offaly. The situation in 1986 is little different from that portrayed for 1991. Perhaps the most significant aspect of the maps is the fact that areas of high *rates* of unemployment are widely dispersed throughout the country and are not restricted to any particular region.

Whilst the identification of these disadvantaged areas (using the unemployment rate criterion) is a valuable exercise, it is essential to draw the distinction between *risk* and *incidence*. When taken in isolation, risk figures (which give the *rate* of unemployment) could give a distorted picture of what is happening on the ground if, for example, a high risk level is derived from a small labour force base. In addition to identifying areas of "high risk", therefore, one must also consider the percentage of the poor who are found in these "high risk" areas. The last four columns of Table 8.1 change the focus from risk to incidence at the county level. Columns 5 and 7 show the distribution of the unemployed across the counties in 1986 and 1991 respectively, while columns 6 and 8 provide a comparable breakdown for the distribution of all persons aged 15 years or more for both years. These latter two distributions may be taken as reference benchmarks against which to measure the degree of concentration or otherwise of the unemployed across the counties. Overall from the table one can see that the distribution of the unemployed is relatively consistent with that of the population aged 15 years and over. Counties or county boroughs which have an over-representation of the unemployed include Limerick County Borough; Donegal; Dublin County Borough; Louth; Waterford County Borough; Wexford and Carlow. There is some evidence to suggest an increase in the degree of over-representation of the unemployed in Dublin County Borough over the study period. For example, in 1986 this area contained 20 per cent of the unemployed compared with 15.6 per cent of the population aged 15 years and over. This corresponds to an over-representation in the order of 28 per cent. By 1991 Dublin County Borough contained 19.8 per cent of the unemployed compared with 14.8 per cent of the population aged 15 years or over — suggesting an over-representation in the order of 34 per cent. Areas which display an under-representation include counties Roscommon, Cavan, Leitrim and also, for example, Dublin, Cork and Limerick counties. In interpreting these figures, it is extremely important to note the effect on the results of the level of aggregation (or so-called Modifiable Areal Unit Problem as discussed in section 8.1 above). For example, although four of the county boroughs experience an over-concentration of the unemployed these are very substantially eroded if one includes the county borough within the overall county area. By doing this for Dublin in 1991, we can see that a total of 33.3 per cent of the unemployed were located in the capital compared with 29.9 per cent of the population aged 15 years and over.

Map 8.1 Unemployment Rates, 1991

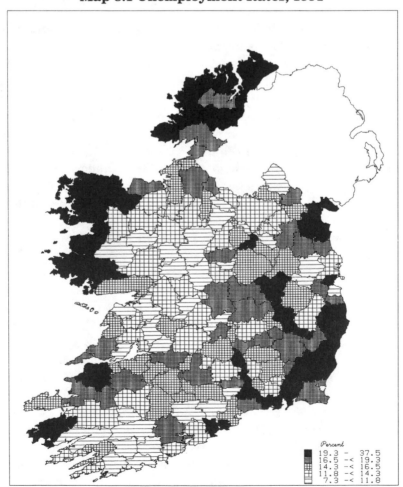

Map 8.2 Unemployment Rates, 1986

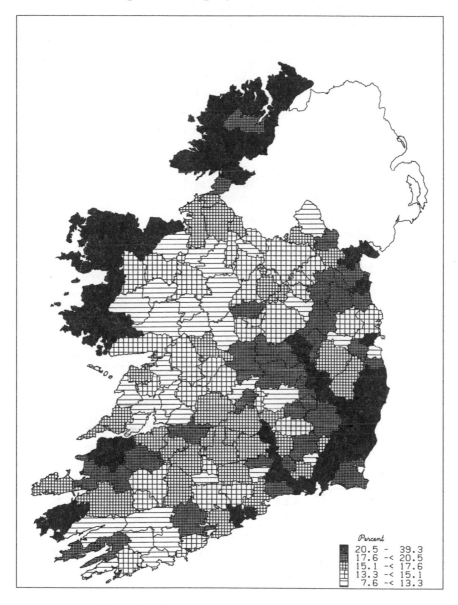

Percent
20.5 - 39.3
17.6 -< 20.5
15.1 -< 17.6
13.3 -< 15.1
7.6 -< 13.3

The county-level data clearly mask a substantial degree of internal variation in unemployment risk and incidence figures at a lower level of spatial disaggregation. To gain some insights into the degree of concentration of the unemployed within the areas of highest risk we group the District Electoral Divisions (DEDs) into deciles on the basis of their unemployment rate. This involves identifying the one-tenth of DEDs with the highest unemployment rates, the next tenth and so on. We then consider the percentage of the unemployed (as well as the percentage of persons aged 15 years and over which acts as a reference benchmark against which to measure degree of concentration) who are contained within the areas defined in terms of these deciles of unemployment rates. The results of this procedure for 1986 and 1991 are presented in Table 8.2.

Table 8.2: Distribution of the Unemployed Classified by Decile of Unemployment Rate at the District Electoral Division Level in 1986 and 1991

Unemployment Rate Decile	Percentage of the Unemployed	Percentage of Population Aged 15+	Percentage of the Unemployed	Percentage of Population Aged 15+
	1986		1991	
Decile 1 (low rate)	2.7	7.1	2.3	6.6
Decile 2	4.3	8.4	3.8	8.0
Decile 3	5.6	9.0	5.1	8.9
Decile 4	6.5	9.2	6.3	9.4
Decile 5	6.4	8.3	6.6	9.0
Decile 6	8.0	9.2	7.5	9.0
Decile 7	9.9	10.3	9.9	10.5
Decile 8	13.1	11.8	12.3	11.3
Decile 9	14.9	11.5	16.1	12.0
Decile 10 (high rate)	28.5	15.1	30.1	15.3
All	100.0	100.0	100.0	100.0

From the table we can see that in 1991 the DEDs in the top decile of unemployment rates[6] contained just over 30 per cent of the unemployed. The same areas (i.e. the same set of DEDs) contained just over 15 per cent of the population aged 15 years or more. This indi-

---

[6] The group of DEDs in each decile are not constrained to be spatially contiguous.

cates an over-representation of the unemployed in this 10 per cent of DEDs with the highest unemployment rates in the order of 97 per cent. One can see, however, that if one's policy objective was to reach a majority of the unemployed by focusing on the areas of highest *rates* one would have to encompass 30 per cent of DEDs in the country (i.e. the top three deciles). This area contains 58 per cent of the unemployed. It should be noted, however, that it also contains 39 per cent of the population aged 15 years and over. This set of areas clearly has more than their "share" of the unemployed (about 49 per cent more than they "should" have if the unemployed were distributed on a pro rata basis with persons aged 15 years and over). Notwithstanding this the figures suggest that if one wished to reach a majority of the unemployed one would have to cover an area which also contained about 40 per cent of the adult population. Once again, the reader is reminded that the areas under discussion are based on decile of unemployment rate with no constraints for spatial contiguity. This means that these areas may be widely distributed across the country.[7]

The figures in Table 8.2 clearly indicate that there has been relatively little change in the decile distributions of both the unemployed and the reference population over the period 1986 to 1991. One can see, for example that if the policy objective in 1986 had been to reach a majority of the unemployed one would have had to include the top three deciles of DEDs defined by their unemployment *rate*. These areas contained 56.5 per cent of the unemployed and 38.4 per cent of persons aged 15 years and over — indicating an over-representation in the order of 47 per cent in 1986 compared with an over-representation of approximately 49 per cent in 1991.

One aspect of the overall picture emerging from the national maps and tables discussed in the chapter to this point is the relatively high degree of constancy in the spatial structure of unemployment over the period 1986 to 1991. A measure of the relationship in the trend between two distributions is given by their so-called correlation coefficient. This is a summary measure of the relationship between two or more variables and can range from −1.0 to +1.0. A coefficient of −1 would imply that there is a perfect negative relationship between two variables (i.e. as one rose the other fell and vice versa). A coefficient of 0 would imply that trends in the two variables in question were unrelated, while a coefficient of +1 would imply that there is a perfect positive relationship between the two variables (i.e. as one increased

---

[7] Indeed, Maps 8.1 and 8.2 indicate that this is in fact the case.

the other increased in exactly the same proportion). To assess the relationship between the spatial structure of unemployment in 1986 and 1991 we can consider the correlation coefficient at the DED level of both the absolute numbers unemployed as well as the unemployment *rate* in 1986 and 1991. When we do this we find that the correlation between absolute numbers unemployed in 1986 and 1991 at the DED level is 0.987 while the correlation in unemployment *rates* is 0.810[8] (both significant at 99 per cent level). These suggest a very strong relationship in the spatial structure of unemployment at the DED level over the two years in question.

In absolute terms, the net change in the numbers of the unemployed at the DED level was relatively small. The DED which experienced the greatest fall in total net unemployment over the period 1986 to 1991 was Finglas South A in which the total number unemployed fell by 187 from 550 in 1986 to 363 in 1991. At the other end of the distribution the DED which experienced the greatest net absolute increase in numbers unemployed over the period was Grace Park (also in Dublin County Borough) where the number unemployed rose by 145 persons from 224 in 1986 to 369 in 1991. Table 8.3 presents details on the overall extent of absolute net change in unemployment across all DEDs in the country. From this, one can see that in 4.3 per cent of DEDs there was no net change in the numbers unemployed. In 45 per cent the net number of unemployed fell by between 1 and 14 persons. Similarly, in just under 31 per cent of DEDs the net number of unemployed rose by the same amount (i.e. between 1 and 14 persons). In general, therefore, Table 8.3 indicates a remarkable constancy in absolute net terms in the numbers of unemployed at the DED level over the period in question.

Analysis of the Census small area data demonstrates beyond argument that high levels of risk of unemployment are not concentrated in particular areas. The extent of targeting possible, using unemployment rate as the screening variable, is quite limited. An extremely strong relationship exists in the spatial structure of unemployment over time.

---

[8] The correlation between *rates* is lower than that between *levels* because in many DEDs the *rates* are based on a relatively small total labour force. Consequently, even a fairly small change in the absolute number of unemployed may result in a disproportionately large change in the *rate* for any given DED. This introduces "noise" into the 1986–1991 comparisons of *rates* which is not apparent in the analysis based on *levels*.

Table 8.3: Absolute Change in the Number of Persons Who Were Classified as Being Unemployed Across all District Electoral Divisions in the Country 1986–1991

Absolute change in Number Unemployed 1986–91	Per Cent of DEDs
−187 to −99	0.3
−98 to −50	1.3
−49 to −25	3.2
−24 to −15	6.7
−14 to −1	44.8
0	4.3
1 to 14	30.6
15 to 24	3.6
25 to 49	2.9
50 to 99	1.8
100 to 145	0.4
Total	100.0

Unemployment — the Dublin Picture

We now change our focus to consider spatial variations in the rate and incidence of unemployment in Dublin City (County Borough) and County.[9] The unemployment rate in Dublin derived from the 1991 Census was 17.8 per cent (77,681 unemployed persons from a labour force of 436,027). The comparable figure for 1986 was 18.5 per cent (77,188 unemployed from a labour force of 416,038). These aggregate figures for both years hide a great deal of internal variation within the capital across the individual wards. In 1991 the ward level unemployment rates ran from a minimum of just under 4 per cent in the Castleknock Park ward to a maximum of 60.5 per cent in the Mountjoy A ward. The degree of variation in unemployment rates can be seen from Table 8.4. This indicates that 22 per cent of wards had an unemployment rate of 9 per cent or less (approximately half the figure for the city and county as a whole). A further 40 per cent of wards had rates ranging from 9 to 18 per cent while 10 per cent of wards

---

[9] There are a total of 322 electoral wards in Dublin City (County Borough) and County. The County Borough contains 162, the County contains 160. The electoral ward in the five county boroughs of Dublin, Galway, Cork, Waterford and Limerick is the equivalent of the district electoral division in the rest of the country.

had a rate of 36 per cent or more (twice the average for the city and
county as a whole). Wards which in 1991 were experiencing extremely high rates of between 55 and 60 per cent included Priorswood
C; North Dock C; Blanchardstown–Mulhuddart; and Priorswood B.
At the other end of the 1991 distribution, wards with particularly low
rates of 4 – 5 per cent included Clonskeagh–Belfield; Firhouse–Bally-
cullen; Rathfarnham Village; Stillorgan–Mount Merrion and Stillorgan–Deerpark.

**Table 8.4: Distribution of Unemployment Rates in the 322
Wards of Dublin City and County in 1986 and 1991**

Unemployment Rate	Percentage of Wards	
	1986	1991
</= 9%	17.7	22.0
>9 to 18%	41.3	39.1
>18 to 27%	19.3	15.8
>27 to 36%	15.2	13.0
>36%	6.5	9.9
All	100.0	100.0

Maps 8.3 and 8.4 show the ward level unemployment rates for Dublin
in 1991 and 1986 respectively. From the former one can see that a
central corridor of wards which experience the highest risk of unemployment stretches from east to west through the County Borough in
the north inner city area from North Dock A, through parts of Bally-
bough and along the quays. To the southside of the city it extends
from the Mansion House A ward, along the quays through parts of
Kilmainham, Crumlin and Drimnagh, stretching into Inchicore, Ballyfermot and Cherry Orchard. There is also an outer ring of high unemployment rate areas in the County Borough, containing parts of
Finglas, Ballymun and Darndale (especially in the Priorswood
wards). To the west of the city boundary this corridor extends with
the county areas into parts of Clondalkin and Tallaght (particularly
the Fettercairn and Jobstown wards). To the north-west we can see
that parts of Blanchardstown — especially the Coolmine, Corduff,
Mulhuddart and Blakestown areas — stand out as having extremely
high rates of unemployment.

A comparison of Maps 8.3 and 8.4 shows that, in general, the
overall spatial structure of the city and county area in terms of unemployment rates remains remarkably constant between 1986 and

1991 with the unemployment "blackspots" of the northern outer rim and central corridor apparent in both years. Trends in the variation of rates throughout the capital were considered in Table 8.4. This showed that the range of rates throughout the wards in the city and county area remained fairly constant over the period 1986 to 1991. The main change seems to be a slight increase in the percentage of wards in the extreme top and bottom categories of the distribution. We can see, for example, that 22 per cent of wards in 1991 had an employment rate of 9 per cent or less. The comparable figure for 1986 was 17.7 per cent. At the top end of the distribution 10 per cent of wards in 1991 had a rate which was double the average compared with a total of 6.5 per cent at this level in 1986. A further measure of spatial trends in unemployment over the period 1986 to 1991 is given by the correlation coefficient in unemployment rates and levels by ward in each of the two years in question. The correlation coefficient between 1986 and 1991 unemployment *rates* at the ward level is 0.95[10], while the coefficient between the *level* (or total number of un-employed) is 0.96 (both significant at the 99 per cent level).

---

[10] The reader's attention is drawn to the fact that there is a much smaller difference between the correlation coefficients based on *rates* and those based on *levels* in Dublin than was the case at the DED Level. The reason for this is that, in general, the labour force in each of the Dublin wards is larger than in DEDs outside the capital. Consequently, Dublin ward level *rates* are not as sensitive to relatively small changes in the absolute level of unemployment as are DEDs elsewhere in the country which have a small labour force base.

Map 8.3: Dublin County and County Borough:
Unemployment Rates, 1991

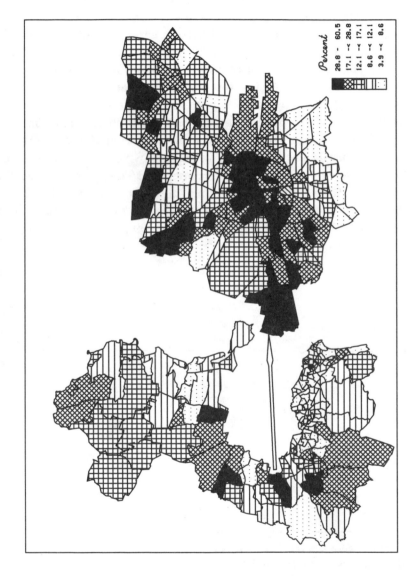

Map 8.4: Dublin County and County Borough: Unemployment Rates, 1986

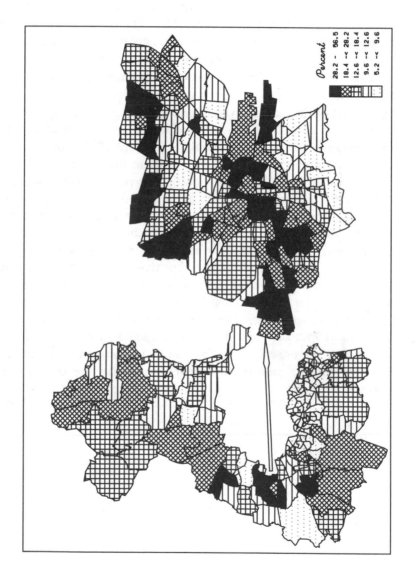

Percent

28.2 - 56.5
18.4 -< 28.2
12.6 -< 18.4
9.6 -< 12.6
5.2 -< 9.6

If we now shift the focus from *rate* of unemployment at ward level to the *incidence* of unemployment we get some insights into the concentration or otherwise of the unemployed across the wards in the city and county areas. Table 8.5 shows the distribution of the unemployed in Dublin across the 322 electoral wards classified into unemployment rate decile for both 1986 and 1991. The comparable distribution of the population aged 15 years or over is also included for both years to act as a reference or benchmark population against which to measure the degree of concentration of unemployment over the area in question. The range of the individual deciles indicate that just over 20 per cent of the unemployed live in those (spatially non-contiguous) wards which constitute the top decile of unemployment rates. This same group of wards contains only 8 per cent of the total population aged 15 years and over. This represents an over-concentration in the wards in question in the order of 154 per cent. In other words, they contain 2½ times as many of the unemployed as they would if the unemployed were distributed across the wards on a pro rata basis with the population aged 15 years and over. Although this indicates a substantial degree of concentration in the wards in question one can see from the table that if one's policy objective were to target over half of the unemployed in Dublin, one would have to encompass all the wards in the top three deciles formed by unemployment rate. These 30 per cent of wards contain 52.6 per cent of the unemployed. They also contain 28.2 per cent of all persons aged 15 years and over. One can see that in general terms there is little change in the incidence of the unemployed across the wards of Dublin city and county between 1986 and 1991.

Table 8.5: Distribution of the Unemployed Classified by Decile of Unemployment Rate at Ward Level for Dublin City and County in 1986 and 1991

Unemployment Rate Decile	1986			1991		
	Range of Decile	Unemployed (per cent)	Population Aged 15yrs + (per cent)	Range of Decile	Unemployed (per cent)	Population Aged 15yrs + (per cent)
Decile 1 (low rate)	5.3–<7.6	3.0	8.7	3.9–<7.2	3.4	10.2
Decile 2	7.6–<9.6	4.7	10.4	7.2–<8.6	4.6	10.7
Decile 3	9.6–<11.4	6.9	12.3	8.6–<10.8	5.7	10.6
Decile 4	11.4–<12.5	7.0	10.5	10.8–<12.1	7.4	11.4
Decile 5	12.5–<15.6	7.9	10.2	12.1–<14.1	8.1	10.6
Decile 6	15.6–<18.2	8.2	9.1	14.1–<16.9	8.9	10.2
Decile 7	18.2–<22.5	10.1	9.1	16.9–<22.8	9.2	8.0
Decile 8	22.5–<28.2	12.6	9.4	22.8–<28.8	15.1	10.4
Decile 9	28.2–<33.5	17.1	10.5	28.8–<35.6	17.4	9.9
Decile 10 (high rate)	33.5–56.4	22.5	9.9	35.6–60.5	20.1	7.9
All		100.0	100.0		100.0	100.0

Notes:

Average unemployment rate in Dublin in 1986 was 18.5 per cent.

Participation rate of 55.8% (416,038 out of 745,533 persons aged 15 years or over).

Average unemployment rate in Dublin in 1991 was 17.8 per cent (77,881 out of a labour force of 436,027).

Participation rate of 56% (436,027 out of 773,047 aged 15 years or over).

The main change in unemployment rates in Dublin involved a slight polarisation with an increased number of households at either end of the spectrum. A central corridor of high unemployment rates can be identified for Dublin. Targeting by unemployment rate would be more effective in Dublin than nationally. However, in order to reach just over one half of the unemployed in Dublin, one would still need to encompass almost three tenths of the persons aged 15 and over.

Social Class

The second proxy for disadvantage and deprivation to be considered is the distribution of persons in the unskilled manual class category. As was the case with unemployment in the previous section the relationship between social class and poverty has been well established. Consequently, by considering spatial variations in the distribution of the unskilled manual class category one can gain a better understanding of the geography of poverty and disadvantage.

Social Class — the National Picture

Table 8.6 presents details on the rate and incidence of the unskilled manual class at the county level in both 1986 and 1991. From this we can see that at a national level a total of 10.4 per cent of persons were classified in this class category in 1991. The highest rate was found in Wexford (almost 15 per cent) followed by Waterford County, Donegal, Carlow and South Tipperary — all with rates in the region of 13–15 per cent. At the other end of the distribution we have Dublin County, Galway County Borough (City area), Roscommon and Sligo — all with rates in the region of 7–8 per cent. In general, there is a high degree of stability between 1986 and 1991 in terms of the rate of the unskilled manual category across the counties. The greatest degree of change seems to have been experienced by Waterford — in both the county and County Borough areas.

The last four columns in the table turn from a consideration of risk to incidence for the unskilled manual category. The reference category of total population is also shown. If the unskilled manual group were distributed across the counties on a pro rata basis with total persons the percentage figures in columns 7 and 8 relating to the 1991 distributions should be largely similar (as should the figures in columns 5 and 6 which relate to the comparable distribution in 1986). From the table one can see that the county distribution of this class category is roughly in line with the distribution of the general population. The greatest *over*-concentrations appear to be in counties Wexford, Donegal, Waterford (both the County and County Borough), South Tipperary, Carlow, Offaly and Dublin County Borough. The highest degree of *under*-concentration is apparent in Galway County Borough, Dublin County and Roscommon. This general picture is largely constant between 1986 and 1991.

Table 8.6: Rates and Incidence of Persons in the Unskilled Manual Class Category by County, 1986 and 1991

| | Percentage in Unskilled Manual Class | | | | Distribution of Persons | | | |
| | 1986 | | 1991 | | 1986 | | 1991 | |
	Per cent	(Rank)	Per cent	(Rank)	Unskilled Manual	Total Population	Unskilled Manual	Total Population
EAST REGION								
Dublin Co. Borough	11.3	(11)	11.1	(14)	15.7	14.2	14.5	13.6
Dublin County	7.0	(31)	6.7	(32)	10.0	14.6	9.9	15.5
Kildare	10.2	(19)	10.2	(21)	3.3	3.3	3.4	3.5
Meath	12.6	(5)	12.0	(8)	3.6	2.9	3.4	3.0
Wicklow	11.6	(8)	11.1	(15)	3.0	2.7	2.9	2.8
SOUTH-WEST REGION								
Cork Co. Borough	10.0	(20)	10.6	(18)	3.7	3.8	3.7	3.6
Cork County	9.1	(23)	10.1	(23)	7.0	7.9	7.8	8.0
Kerry	11.1	(13)	11.8	(9)	3.8	3.5	3.9	3.5
WEST REGION								
Galway Co. Borough	6.9	(32)	6.7	(31)	0.9	1.3	0.9	1.4
Galway County	8.6	(28)	9.9	(26)	3.1	3.7	3.5	3.7
Mayo	9.7	(21)	9.9	(25)	3.1	3.2	3.0	3.1
MIDLANDS REGION								
Laois	12.3	(6)	11.1	(13)	1.8	1.5	1.6	1.5
Longford	10.3	(18)	10.3	(20)	0.9	0.9	0.9	0.9
Offaly	13.4	(4)	13.0	(6)	2.2	1.7	2.1	1.7
Westmeath	10.5	(15)	10.0	(24)	1.8	1.8	1.7	1.8
Roscommon	8.2	(29)	7.5	(30)	1.2	1.5	1.1	1.5

Table 8.6: Rates and Incidence of Persons in the Unskilled Manual Class Category by County, 1986 and 1991

| | Percentage in Unskilled Manual Class | | | | Distribution of Persons | | | |
| | 1986 | | 1991 | | 1986 | | 1991 | |
	Per cent	(Rank)	Per cent	(Rank)	Unskilled Manual	Total Population	Unskilled Manual	Total Population
SOUTH-EAST REGION								
Carlow	13.6	(3)	13.7	(4)	1.5	1.2	1.5	1.2
Kilkenny	11.4	(10)	10.7	(16)	2.3	2.1	2.1	2.1
Wexford	14.7	(1)	14.7	(1)	4.2	4.1	4.1	2.9
South Tipperary	12.0	(7)	13.3	(5)	2.6	2.7	2.7	2.1
Waterford Co. Borough	8.6	(27)	12.8	(7)	0.9	1.4	1.4	1.1
Waterford County	11.2	(12)	14.7	(2)	1.6	2.1	2.1	1.4
NORTH-EAST REGION								
Louth	11.5	(9)	11.4	(12)	2.9	2.6	2.8	2.6
Cavan	8.8	(25)	10.5	(19)	1.3	1.5	1.5	1.5
Monaghan	8.8	(26)	9.4	(27)	1.3	1.5	1.3	1.4
MID-WEST REGION								
Clare	9.3	(22)	10.2	(22)	2.3	2.6	2.5	2.6
Limerick Co. Borough	10.3	(17)	11.7	(10)	1.6	1.6	1.7	1.5
Limerick County	11.1	(14)	10.6	(17)	3.3	3.1	3.2	3.1
North Tipperary	10.4	(16)	11.5	(11)	1.7	1.7	1.8	1.6
NORTH-WEST REGION								
Leitrim	9.0	(24)	9.3	(28)	0.7	0.8	0.6	0.7
Sligo	8.1	(30)	8.4	(29)	1.2	1.6	1.3	1.5
Donegal	14.1	(2)	14.3	(3)	5.1	3.7	5.0	3.6
State	10.2	–	10.4	–	100	100	100	100

Maps 8.5 and 8.6 present the rate of the unskilled manual class category at the rural/urban district level. Map 8.5 shows that in 1991 the districts with the highest rates of their population in this class grouping were found in parts of Donegal, north and west Mayo, Galway, north Kerry and parts of the south-east running through counties Waterford, South Tipperary and Kilkenny as well as Wexford, Wicklow and Kildare. The same pattern is generally apparent from Map 8.6 relating to 1986.

Map 8.5: Percentage Unskilled Manual, 1991

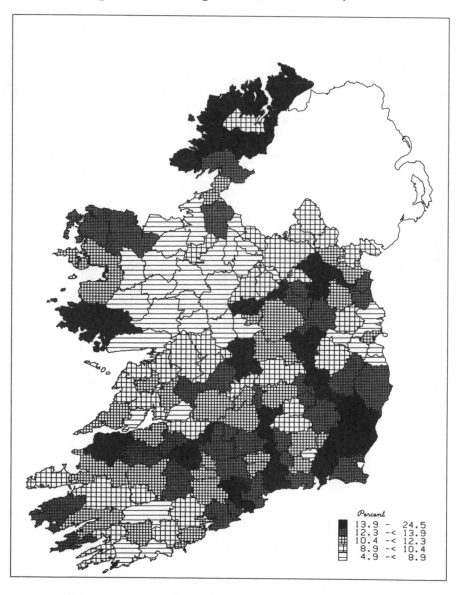

Map 8.6: Percentage Unskilled Manual, 1986

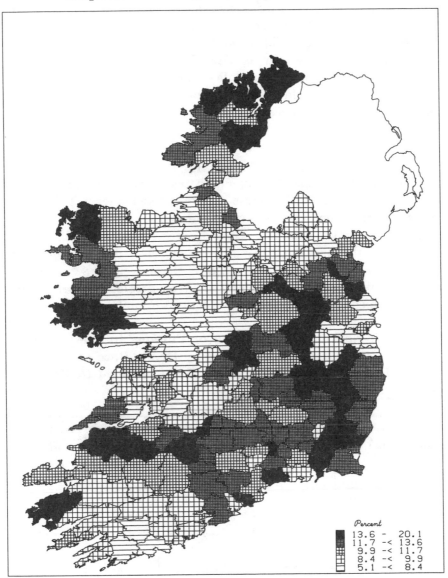

Percent

13.6 - 20.1
11.7 -< 13.6
9.9 -< 11.7
8.4 -< 9.9
5.1 -< 8.4

Perhaps one of the most striking aspects of these maps is the relative absence of districts with a high percentage of their population in the unskilled manual group in parts of counties Roscommon, Longford, Mayo, Sligo, Leitrim and Cavan. This is largely attributable to the importance of farmers, particularly small farmers, in the occupational structure of the areas in question. The Census classification

assigns farmers to social class according to size of farm. Small farmers (less than 30 acres) are assigned to the semi-skilled manual category. No farmers (of any size) are assigned to the unskilled manual
category. The highest incidence of small farmers is in the Roscommon, Leitrim and Cavan areas. This means that, by definition, such
people do not fall into the unskilled manual class category. Consequently, there is a relative absence of districts in the counties in
question with a high percentage of their population classified as unskilled manual.

To provide an insight into the degree of concentration or otherwise
at a sub-county level, Table 8.7 presents details on the incidence or
distribution of the unskilled manual category according to its decile
distribution of *rates* at the district electoral division level. This allows
one to examine the percentage of the class group which is distributed
across the country according to the deciles formed by DED *rate* of
persons in the unskilled manual category. The distribution of all
adults according to the areas formed by these decile *rates* of the unskilled manual group is also presented as a reference benchmark
against which to measure the degree of over- or under-concentration.

**Table 8.7: National Distribution of Persons in the Unskilled
Manual Class Category Classified by Decile Rate of Unskilled
Manual at the District Electoral Division Level in 1986 and
1991**

Unemployment Rate Decile	Percentage of the Unskilled Manual	Percentage of Total Population	Percentage of the Unskilled Manual	Percentage of Total Population
	1986		1991	
Decile 1 (low rate)	3.7	13.8	3.7	13.6
Decile 2	5.4	10.5	5.7	10.8
Decile 3	6.0	9.2	7.0	10.5
Decile 4	7.1	9.1	7.0	8.7
Decile 5	8.7	9.6	9.4	10.0
Decile 6	11.4	11.0	9.8	9.3
Decile 7	11.0	9.3	11.3	9.4
Decile 8	12.3	9.0	14.8	10.9
Decile 9	16.7	10.2	13.2	8.1
Decile 10 (high rate)	17.6	8.2	18.0	8.6
All	100.0	100.0	100.0	100.0

From the third column in the table, one can see that 18 per cent of the unskilled manual group were located in the 10 per cent of DEDs with the highest rate of unskilled manual persons. This same set of areas contained a total of 9 per cent of the total population. The top three deciles in 1991 contained 46 per cent of persons from the unskilled manual class category compared with 28 per cent of all persons. At the other end of the distribution one can see, for example, that only 4 per cent of the group in question are contained within the areas formed by the lowest decile of *rates*, compared with 14 per cent of the total population.

Definitional aspects of social class ensure that areas with large numbers of farmers have a low percentage of their population classified as unskilled manual. The value of social class as a screening variable is only slightly greater than unemployment. For both, the ratio of unemployed persons or persons in the unskilled manual class to the total numbers of persons aged 15 and over, by taking the top three deciles, is just in excess of one and a half to one.

Social Class — the Dublin Picture

We now turn to consider spatial variations in the unskilled manual category in Dublin. Maps 8.7 and 8.8 show the percentage of persons in each ward assigned to the unskilled manual group. In 1991 rates varied from a low of under one per cent in Terenure C to a high of 32 per cent in the Merchant's Quay A ward. Map 8.7 identifies a central corridor of high rates, running through the inner city County Borough area with an outer ring in parts of Finglas, Ballymun and Darndale. In the North County area (Fingal) we can see a tract of high rate wards running north-south through parts of Swords, through Hollywood, Naul and Balscadden to the North. In the South County area, parts of Tallaght, Firhouse and Bohernabreena stand out as having extremely high rates of their population in the unskilled manual class. A comparison of Maps 8.7 and 8.8 shows that, in general, the spatial distribution of the unskilled manual category in Dublin remains relatively unchanged between 1986 and 1991. The central corridor and outer northern ring of the County Borough area is apparent in both years as are the high risk areas in the North County (Fingal) and South County region in Tallaght and Bohernabreena. A statistical measure of the constancy in the spatial structure of this class category over the period in question is given by the correlation coefficient between 1986 and 1991 for both the total *numbers* and the *percentage* of persons in the unskilled manual group. The correlation between the percentages over the two years in question is 0.72 while that between the total *number* of persons (i.e. between the levels) is 0.97 — both coefficients significant at the 99 per cent level. This indicates a high degree of consistency in the spatial structure of this segment of the population over the period in question.

A further comparison of Maps 8.7 and 8.8 can be made with Maps 8.3 and 8.4 on unemployment. It is clear from visual inspection that there is a positive relationship between the distribution of the unemployed and the unskilled manual group in the capital. A measure of this relationship is given by the correlation at the ward level between the unemployment rate and the percentage of the population in the unskilled manual category in each of the years in question. In 1986 the relevant coefficient stood at 0.875 while in 1991 it was 0.856 (both significant at the 99 per cent level) indicating a strong relationship between the spatial structures of unemployment and the unskilled manual class category in Dublin in both years.

Map 8.7: Dublin County and County Borough:
Percentage in Unskilled Manual Class, 1991

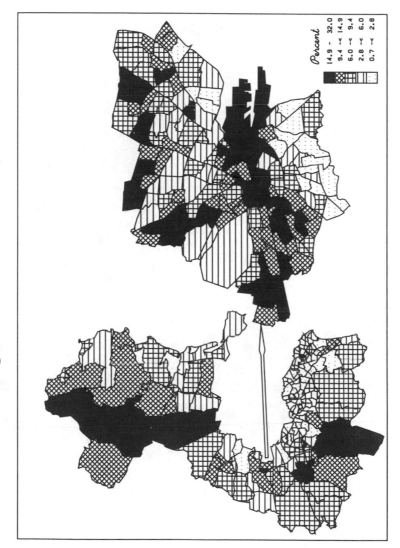

Percent

14.9 – 32.0
9.4 –< 14.9
6.0 –< 9.4
2.8 –< 6.0
0.7 –< 2.8

Map 8.8: Dublin County and County Borough:
Percentage in Unskilled Manual Class, 1986

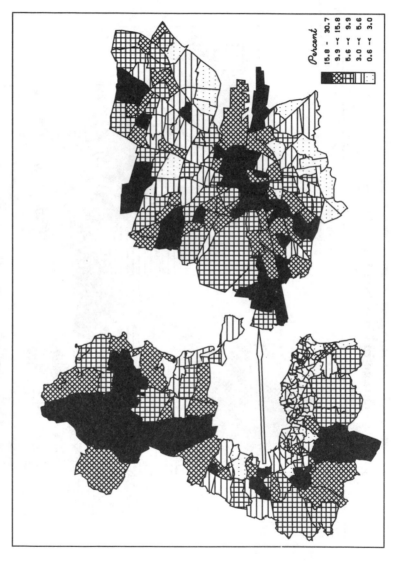

Table 8.8: Distribution of Persons in the Unskilled Manual Class Category Classified by Decile Rate of Unskilled Manual at Ward level for Dublin City and County in 1986 and 1991

Unemployment Rate Decile	Percentage of the Unskilled Manual	Percentage of Total Population	Percentage of the Unskilled Manual	Percentage of Total Population
	1986		1991	
Decile 1 (low rate)	1.3	8.9	1.4	8.6
Decile 2	2.5	9.6	2.6	10.1
Decile 3	4.9	11.8	5.0	11.4
Decile 4	6.2	11.5	6.0	10.5
Decile 5	7.5	10.7	8.9	12.0
Decile 6	7.5	8.1	9.4	9.6
Decile 7	12.1	9.7	11.8	10.0
Decile 8	17.5	11.0	16.7	10.3
Decile 9	20.8	10.8	16.2	8.4
Decile 10 (high rate)	19.7	7.9	22.0	8.6
All	100.0	100.0	100.0	100.0

Turning from rate to incidence, as before we look at the distribution of the unskilled manual category according to the areas formed by the decile rate distribution to assess the degree of concentration (or otherwise) within the areas of highest/lowest rates. The information is presented in Table 8.8. From this one can see that in 1991 the 10 per cent of wards with the highest rates of the unskilled manual group in their population contained a total of 22 per cent of the unskilled manual group compared with 9 per cent of all persons as a whole. Wards in the top three deciles contained 55 per cent of the unskilled manual class, compared with 27 per cent of all persons — indicating an over-representation in the order of 97 per cent. At the other end of the distribution the 10 per cent of DEDs with the lowest *rates* of the unskilled manual class accounted for 1.4 per cent of persons in that class category compared with 8.6 per cent of all persons as a whole. The 30 per cent of wards in the capital with the lowest *rates* for the unskilled manual group contained 9 per cent of the category and 30 per cent of all persons. The figures in the table show that there has been little change in terms of the incidence of the unskilled manual group over the period 1986 to 1991.

An extremely strong correlation exists between unemployment and social class in Dublin. However, targeting by social class proves to be somewhat easier. By focusing on the top three deciles we can identify a majority of the unskilled manual class in comparison with one in four households overall.

Local Authority Rental Housing

The final proxy for deprivation which will be considered is the distribution of private permanent households which are rented from the local authority. In the Census form, households are asked about the nature of their housing tenure, and here we focus on those who said that they were renting from the local authority.

Local Authority Rental Housing — the National Picture

The number of households rented from the local authority expressed as a percentage of the total number of permanent private households in the area provides what we refer to as the local authority rental rate for the area. This information was not collected in 1986 and the subsequent analysis therefore relates to 1991 only. The national distribution of this social housing rental rate is shown in Map 8.9. We see that districts with the highest rates of local authority rentals are, in general, found in the East and South-East of the country with outliers in Stranorlar (Donegal); Ballina (Mayo); Listowel and Tralee (Kerry); Ballymahon and Longford (Longford). The main concentration of areas with a high rate of local authority rentals runs through parts of Tipperary, Kilkenny, Carlow, Waterford, Wexford, Wicklow, Kildare and Dublin.

Map 8.9: Percentage Private Permanent Households
Rented from Local Authority, 1991

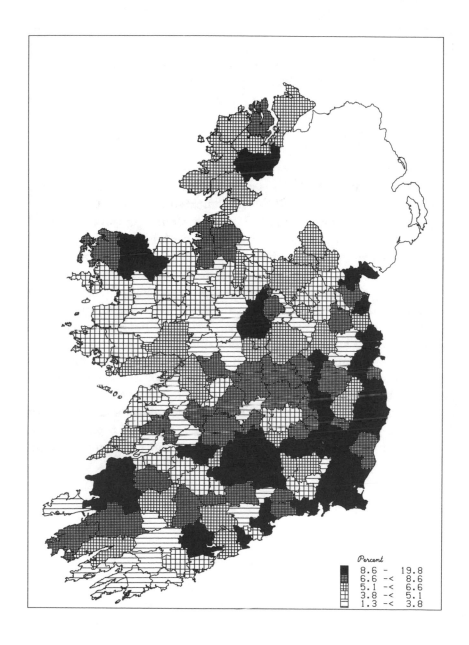

Percent

■	8.6 - 19.8
	6.6 -< 8.6
	5.1 -< 6.6
	3.8 -< 5.1
□	1.3 -< 3.8

Table 8.9 provides details on the county level *rates* of social housing. At the national level this stands at 9.7% in 1991. Table 8.9 shows that the highest rates of local authority rented housing are in the County Boroughs of Limerick, Waterford, Cork and Dublin — with figures in the region of 17–19 per cent of all private permanent households. These areas are followed by South Tipperary, Dublin County, Louth, Wexford, Wicklow and Longford, all 9–12 per cent. Information on the distribution of local authority rentals is provided in the second column of the table. This shows, for example, that 27 per cent of rented social housing is found in Dublin County Borough, a further 16 per cent in Dublin county and so on. The distribution of a benchmark or reference population of all households is shown in the fourth column of the table. This clearly shows that there is a sizeable *over*-concentration of local authority rentals in the four County Boroughs mentioned. For example, Limerick County Borough contains exactly 100 per cent more social housing rentals than would be the case if the latter were distributed across the counties on a pro rata basis with the population of all households. Similarly, Cork County Borough has an over-concentration of 86.5 per cent; Dublin County Borough an over-concentration of exactly 75 per cent and so on. Although the County Borough area clearly displays this over-concentration, it should be pointed out that if one considers Dublin as a whole, the County and County Borough contains 43.6 per cent of local authority rentals compared with 30.4 per cent of all private permanent households. Comparable figures for Cork are 10.9 per cent of rented social housing and 11.6 per cent of all households; Waterford 3.1 per cent and 2.5 per cent and Limerick 4.6 per cent and 4.5 per cent respectively.[11] There are substantially smaller over-concentrations in the relevant county areas.

---

[11] As noted previously in the chapter this clearly highlights the so-called modifiable areal unit problem encountered in analysing area-based data.

Table 8.9: Rates and Incidence of Local Authority Rentals by County, 1991

	Local Authority Rental Rate	(Rank)	% of L.A. Rentals	% of All Households
EAST REGION				
Dublin Co. Borough	17.0	(4)	27.3	15.6
Dublin County	10.7	(6)	16.3	14.8
Kildare	6.5	(19)	2.1	3.2
Meath	5.8	(22)	1.7	2.8
Wicklow	9.9	(9)	2.8	2.7
SOUTH-WEST REGION				
Cork Co. Borough	18.1	(3)	6.9	3.7
Cork County	4.9	(30)	4.0	7.9
Kerry	8.2	(13)	3.0	3.5
SOUTH-EAST REGION				
Carlow	8.5	(12)	0.9	1.1
Kilkenny	7.6	(16)	1.6	2.0
Wexford	10.2	(8)	2.9	2.8
South Tipperary	11.1	(5)	2.4	2.1
Waterford Co. Borough	18.9	(2)	2.2	1.1
Waterford County	6.3	(21)	0.9	1.4
NORTH-EAST REGION				
Louth	10.7	(7)	2.8	2.5
Cavan	5.1	(29)	0.8	1.5
Monaghan	5.5	(25)	0.8	1.4
MID-WEST REGION				
Clare	5.8	(24)	1.5	2.6
Limerick Co. Borough	19.1	(1)	3.0	1.5
Limerick County	5.3	(26)	1.6	3.0
North Tipperary	8.1	(14)	1.3	1.6
MIDLANDS REGION				
Laois	6.6	(17)	0.9	1.4
Longford	9.0	(10)	0.8	0.9
Offaly	7.7	(15)	1.2	1.6
Westmeath	5.2	(28)	0.9	1.7
Roscommon	3.6	(32)	0.6	1.5
WEST REGION				
Galway Co. Borough	8.9	(11)	1.3	1.4
Galway County	4.4	(31)	1.6	3.5
Mayo	5.3	(27)	1.7	3.2
NORTH-WEST REGION				
Leitrim	5.8	(23)	0.5	0.8
Sligo	6.6	(18)	1.1	1.6
Donegal	6.4	(20)	2.3	3.5
State	9.7	−	100.0	100.0

The degree of concentration of local authority rentals at the sub-county (DED) level is shown in Table 8.10. This focuses on the national incidence of the group in question according to its decile distribution of *rates*. From the table one can see that the bottom two deciles of rates have been combined. This was necessary because a total of 18 per cent of DEDs (618) in the country contain no local authority rentals at all. From this one can see, for example, that two-thirds of all local authority rentals are contained in the DEDs which fell within the decile of areas with the highest rental rates. This compares with the 23 per cent of all households which were encompassed by this same set of DEDs, implying that almost three times as many local authority rental households are found in these areas as would be the case if local authority rentals were distributed across all areas on a pro rata basis with all households in the country. The top two deciles of high rate DEDs are seen to contain 82 per cent of local authority rentals compared with 37 per cent of all households. The degree of concentration provided by the local authority housing variable at the level of the DED is thus substantially higher than was found for either the unemployed or unskilled manual distributions discussed above.

Table 8.10: National Distribution of Local Authority Rentals Classified by Decile Rental Rate at the DED Level in 1991

L.A. Rate Decile	Local Authority Rentals	All Households	The Unemployed	Population Aged 15 yrs+
	Per Cent			
Decile 1 & 2 (low rate)	0.1	14.3	8.0	14.0
Decile 3	0.7	8.7	5.7	8.8
Decile 4	1.0	6.3	4.5	6.3
Decile 5	1.6	6.7	4.9	6.7
Decile 6	2.7	7.8	6.5	7.9
Decile 7	4.0	8.1	7.3	8.1
Decile 8	7.9	10.9	10.6	10.9
Decile 9	16.1	14.6	15.8	14.7
Decile 10 (high rate)	65.8	22.6	36.7	22.4
Total	100.0	100.0	100.0	100.0

The final two columns of Table 8.10 show the distributions of the un-employed as well as the adult population according to the decile rate distribution of local authority rental households. In other words, the table shows, for example, the percentage of persons in the country who are unemployed and who fall within the area formed by the 10 per cent of DEDs with the highest rates of local authority rental housing, the 10 per cent of DEDs with the next highest rate of local authority rentals and so on. The distribution of the adult population (aged 15 years and over) according to the classification based on local authority rental rates is also shown. From this we can see that a total of 37 per cent of the unemployed in the country are found within the 10 per cent of DEDs with the highest local authority rental rates compared with 22 per cent of the adult population. Just over one-half (52 per cent) of the national total of unemployed fall within the top two deciles of the local authority rental rate distribution compared with 37 per cent of the adult population.

Local authority housing is heavily concentrated in the five county boroughs. Targeting by local authority rentals presents no difficulty with two-thirds of such households being captured by the highest decile. In fact, the local authority rental measure is almost as effec-tive in targeting as the measure itself.

Local Authority Rental Housing — the Dublin Picture

Turning to Dublin, there is a great deal of variation in the local authority rental rate across the 322 wards. A total of 34 wards (11 per cent in the County and County Borough area) contain no local authority rentals at all while a further 55 wards have a public sector rental rate of less than 1 per cent. In a total of 127 wards the rate is more than 10 per cent and in 17 wards it is in excess of 70 per cent. These high rate areas include Priorswood C and Ushers B (each with a rate of 94 per cent), Tallaght–Fettercairn and Merchants Quay A (each with a rate of 92 per cent), Ballymun D (90 per cent) and Cherry Orchard C (86 per cent).

These areas with high rates are shown on Map 8.10.

Map 8.10: Dublin County and County Borough: Percentage Private
Permanent Households Rented from Local Authority, 1991

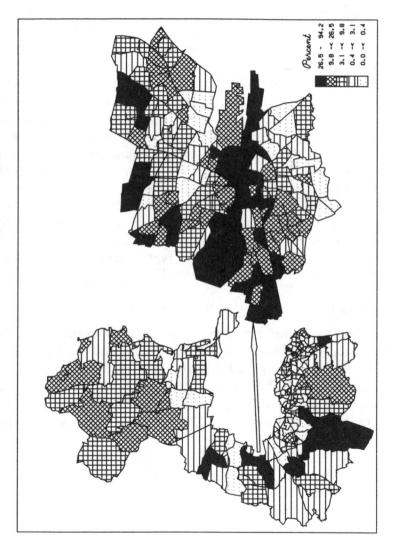

Percent

26.5 – 94.2
9.8 –< 26.5
3.1 –< 9.8
0.4 –< 3.1
0.0 –< 0.4

From this we can see that the areas with the highest rates of rented social housing run westwards from North Dock B, through the North and South central inner city wards to Ballyfermot and Cherry Orchard wards. On the northern rim of the County Borough we can see areas with high rates in the local authority rental sector in parts of Finglas, Ballymun and Darndale. In the county area one can see that parts of Blanchardstown (particularly Tyrrelstown, Mulhuddart and Coolmine); Clondalkin; and Tallaght (Fettercairn, Jobstown, Killinarden) stand out with rates in the highest quintile of the distribution.

Table 8.11 provides details on the distribution of local authority housing in Dublin according to the areas formed by its decile rate distribution, along with the distribution of all households and also the distribution of the unemployed and the population aged 15 years or over. One can see from the table that the bottom two deciles contain only 0.1 per cent of rented social housing compared with 19.5 per cent of all households. The second decile contains 0.5 per cent of local authority rentals (compared with 11 per cent of all households) and so on. At the top end of the distribution one can see that 43 per cent of local authority rentals in Dublin City and County are contained within the top 10 per cent of wards sorted by rate of rented social housing. This same group of wards contains 9 per cent of all households in the capital. This indicates that they have almost 5 times as many local authority rentals as they would if such rentals were distributed on a pro rata basis with all households in Dublin as a whole. When the top two deciles of DEDs are considered together we can see they contain 67 per cent of rented social housing compared with 19 per cent of all households.

Table 8.11: Distribution of Local Authority Rentals in Dublin City and County Classified by Decile Rental Rate at the Ward Level in 1991

L.A. Rate Decile	Percentage of:			
	Local Authority Rentals	All Households	The Unemployed	Population Aged 15 yrs+
Decile 1 & 2 (low rate)	0.1	19.5	8.7	18.8
Decile 3	0.5	10.8	6.7	11.0
Decile 4	1.8	11.5	7.6	11.9
Decile 5	3.0	10.3	7.3	10.2
Decile 6	5.2	9.7	8.6	10.4
Decile 7	8.4	9.8	10.4	9.8
Decile 8	13.8	9.7	13.3	9.7
Decile 9	24.0	9.8	17.2	9.9
Decile 10 (high rate)	43.3	8.9	20.1	8.2
Total	100.0	100.0	100.0	100.0

The final two columns in Table 8.11 provide information on the distribution of both the unemployed population and also the total population aged 15 years and over according to the same geographical classification of wards. The distribution of adults acts as a reference category for the population of the unemployed. From the data, one can see that the top 10 per cent of Wards sorted by *rate* of local authority rentals contains 20 per cent of unemployed persons compared with 8 per cent of all adults, while the top 20 per cent of wards classified in this way contains 37 per cent of the unemployed compared with 18 per cent of all adults. In interpreting these figures it is important to note that the information on the numbers and rate of unemployed referred to *all* unemployed persons. If details on unemployed heads of household or on the long-term unemployed were available from the Census one might well have found that the percentage of these two sub-categories of the unemployed which could be reached in the top deciles of wards using the local authority rental rate criterion might well have been higher than the 37 per cent presented in Table 8.11.

Conclusions

The Census SAPS does not contain a measure of poverty and deprivation. It does, however, allow us to map a number of socio-demographic characteristics which we know from other sources to be good predictors of poverty at the household level. The most important proxies or surrogates of poverty available in the SAPS data are unemployment, social class and household tenure. With regard to unemployment the most striking finding is the fact that high rates are not concentrated in any particular set of regions. The three deciles with the highest rates, which include almost six out of ten of the unemployed, also contain four out of ten of all households. Concentration of unemployment is greater in Dublin but only marginally so. One can, however, identify a central corridor and northern outer rim of wards in Dublin which experience particularly high rates of unemployment. These unemployment "blackspots" have remained relatively stable over time although there has been a slight tendency towards polarisation.

Unskilled manual workers are also widely distributed spatially although the definition of employed ensures that they are largely absent from areas where farming is particularly important. Few significant variations were observed over time. As a consequence its potential as a screening variable for selective policies is no greater than unemployment; although concentration is again slightly higher in Dublin. Local authority tenancy is associated with very high levels of spatial concentration. Two-thirds of local authority rentals are concentrated in the top decile with the highest rental rates, and eight out of ten are found in the top two. These figures are respectively three times and over two times higher than we would expect on the basis of the overall distribution of households. In Dublin, concentration is a good deal greater, with the top decile accounting for over four out of ten local authority rentals. This figure is five times higher than we would predict solely on the basis of population size. This set of households also contains one fifth of the unemployed, a figure two and a half times that which we would observe on the basis of a proportionate distribution of unemployment.

Chapter 9

Conclusions

Introduction

Our preceding analysis has focused on what can be learnt from taking a spatial perspective on disadvantage and deprivation by making use of the 1987 and 1994 Living in Ireland Surveys, and the 1986 and 1991 Census SAPS data. The aim has been to examine what types of areas had particularly high rates of poverty, the extent to which poor and disadvantaged people were concentrated in particular areas, and whether such patterns had changed over time.

The Results from Survey Data

Using the two household surveys, the risk of poverty was seen to have fallen for households located in open country areas between 1987 and 1994, while it rose for those in Dublin city and county. At both points in time the highest risk of poverty was observed for villages and towns with populations of less than three thousand. While the proportion of the poor located in Dublin increased significantly over the period, the number of poor households found there is still, at most, only as high as its share in the overall population. Poverty is not, to any significant degree, concentrated in any of the area types which we could identify in the surveys. Housing tenure is a more significant factor in explaining the distribution of poverty risks and the concentration of poverty than location *per se*. Particularly, high risks of poverty are associated with being a local authority tenant, and between 1987 and 1994 the level of risk for such households increased significantly. Local authority tenant-purchasers, although significantly less disadvantaged, still suffered risk levels well above average and saw a significant deterioration in their situation between 1987 and 1994. Despite their increasing risk of poverty, households in public sector housing did not account for a greater proportion of the

poor in 1994 because the numbers in such housing fell. Using as poverty standard the 60 per cent relative income line combined with basic deprivation, local authority renters made up just about forty per
cent of the poor in both 1987 and 1994 and public housing overall (including tenant purchase) made up about one half.

Focusing on this combined income and deprivation measure, we
proceeded to examine whether tenure had an impact which varied
with location in an urban centre or elsewhere. Over the 1987-1994
period we observed a significant increase in the risk of poverty for
local authority households in Dublin city and county, which brought
it up to the rates for similar households in other urban centres. The
extremely low rate of poverty in non-local authority housing in Dublin city and county means that the differential between the two types
of tenure is greater there than elsewhere and it is this juxtaposition
of extreme poverty and affluence which gives urban centres their distinctive profile. This polarisation is accentuated in Dublin because
particularly high rates are observed for local authority renters compared to tenant-purchasers; in Dublin, almost seven out of ten
households renting local authority housing fall below the poverty
line. By 1994, one in five poor households were located in local
authority housing in Dublin city and county. Local authority households in urban centres more broadly comprise just over one in nine of
all households but contain three out of ten poor households. However,
it still remains true that one in two poor households are located outside public sector housing.

The study then sought to address the question of whether variations in risk of poverty by location and tenure are primarily a consequence of differences between households in terms of factors such as
education and labour market experience. We found that, to a large
extent, the disadvantages experienced by local authority households,
and their accentuation over the 1987 to 1994 period, are indeed accounted for by the socio-demographic make-up of the households involved. Local authority rental households, for instance, are more
likely to be poor because the head of household has a higher probability of being from the unskilled manual class, being poorly edu-
cated, unemployed, without a partner, and so on. Deterioration of
their position over time arises both because factors, in relation to
which they are disadvantaged, such as education and unemployment,
increase in importance over time; and because the profile displayed
by these households, in relation to features, such as education, long-
term unemployment and presence of a partner, deteriorates over
time.

However, even when we control for a range of such socio-demographic influences urban local authority tenants in 1994 still display an odds-ratio relating to risk of poverty which is six times higher than that relating to urban outright owners and mortgage holders. Nevertheless, we have cautioned against assuming that such residual effects can be entirely attributed to tenure or a combination of tenure and location and have signalled our intention to pursue this further.

Further evidence of the limited nature of spatial concentration of deprivation and disadvantage was given by our analysis of poverty by planning region in the 1987 and 1994 surveys. Over time a decline occurred in the poverty rates for the North-West and Donegal and the West. As a consequence the difference between the East and other regions were eroded, producing a striking consistency in poverty rates across regions. The extent of concentration of poverty by region is so minimal by 1994 that we could substitute the figures for the overall distribution of households for those relating to incidence without introducing any significant distortion.

Evidence from Census Data

Analysis of the highly disaggregated Census SAPS data for 1986 and 1991 showed results consistent with the conclusions deriving from our survey analysis. To provide a more spatially disaggregated insight into the risk and incidence of deprivation and disadvantage we presented an analysis of the spatial concentration of unemployment, social class and social housing using the 1986 and 1991 Small Area Population Statistics[1]. When discussing unemployment we saw that the counties with the highest rates include Donegal, Louth and Dublin County Borough, while Roscommon, Cavan, Clare and Leitrim had relatively lower rates. (The importance of taking small-scale farming into account when interpreting the low unemployment rates in these counties was noted.) Despite this variation in unemployment rates, the distribution of the unemployed by county corresponded reasonably closely to that of the adult population. In 1991 Dublin city and county as a whole contained one-third of the unemployed, compared with 30 per cent of the population aged 15 years and over. The 10 per cent of DEDs with the highest unemployment rates contained

---

[1] Information on social housing was not collected in the 1986 Census therefore analysis of social housing relates to 1991 only.

30 per cent of the unemployed, compared with 15 per cent of the adult population. The top 30 per cent of DEDs contained 51 per cent of the unemployed versus 39 per cent of the adult population. Focusing on Dublin city and county, a central corridor of DEDs with high unemployment rates was identified running through the inner city wards, and high rates were also seen in parts of Finglas, Ballymun, Darndale, Crumlin, Inchicore and Ballyfermot, in Clondalkin and Tallaght, and in parts of Blanchardstown, Coolmine, Corduff, Mulhuddart and Blakestown. The 30 per cent of wards with the highest unemployment rates were found to contain 52 per cent of the unemployed and 28 per cent of the adult population.

The second Census variable considered was the unskilled manual class category. We saw that Wexford, Donegal, Waterford and Carlow were the counties with the highest percentage of their population in this social group. The distribution of the unskilled manual category at the county level largely corresponds with the distribution of the adult population. In 1991 the 30 per cent of DEDs with the highest percentage of their population in the unskilled manual group contained 46 per cent of persons in that class category, compared with 28 per cent of all persons. In Dublin, we saw that a central corridor of DEDs with a high proportion of their populations in this class ran through the county borough area with an outer ring of high rates in wards in parts of Finglas, Ballymun, and Darndale. Within Dublin we saw that the 30 per cent of DEDs with the highest percentage in that class contained 55 per cent of persons in the Unskilled Manual category compared with 27 per cent of all persons.

Finally, the location of households renting from local authorities was examined. At a national level rural/urban districts with the highest rates of rented social housing were found in the south and east of the country. At a county level, local authority rentals were distributed largely in line with the distribution of all households. The exception was Dublin with a substantial over-concentration of local authority rentals: it contained approximately 75 per cent more than would be found if local authority rentals had been distributed on a pro rata basis with all households. The 20 per cent of DEDs with the highest proportion of their households renting from the local authority contained a total of 67 per cent of all local authority rented households versus 19 per cent of all households, and so had more than three and a half times as many local authority rentals as would be found if they had been distributed on a pro rata basis with all households. Within Dublin we found a central corridor of wards with a high rate of local authority households running from west to east through the County Borough area, and in parts of Finglas, Ballymun and Darndale, and in parts of Blanchardstown, Clondalkin and Tallaght. The 20 per cent of Dublin wards with the highest proportions of local authority renters contained 82 per cent of all local authority rentals in Dublin compared with only 27 per cent of all households.

Methodological Issues

In our discussion of the SAPS data we choose not to create an aggregated measure of deprivation. Earlier work by Haase, McKeown and Rourke (1996) has sought to use the SAPS data to identify dimensions of "deprivation" and, in turn, derive an aggregated deprivation score from these measures. The difficulty with such a procedure is that the Census data does not contain a measure of income or satisfactory measures of deprivation. The available variables relate, almost entirely, to socio-demographic characteristics such as social class, education, unemployment and tenure. One can identify dimensions of socio-demographic structure, subject to the usual arguments about the adequacy of the sample of indicators and the appropriateness of the final choice of labels. However, the weights derived from such an analysis can be informative only with regard to the relationships between the socio-demographic variables but not to the association between such variables and deprivation or poverty. In other words, we can establish how closely social class and education are related to each other, at this level of aggregation, but if we were to establish that they were more closely related to each other than to unemployment this would not imply that they were both more accurate predictors of poverty than unemployment. We do not possess, nor can we create, solely on the basis of the Census data, anything comparable to a set of regression weights which, in some measurable sense, would provide a best estimate of a poverty rate. Consequently, there is no way in which we can establish that any mapping of deprivation based on the weights derived from a factor analysis of a set of socio-demographic characteristics is superior to that based on the weights from any other such analysis. If any such mapping does provide an adequate approximation to the spatial distribution of deprivation it must inevitably be in spite of — rather than because of — the application of arbitrary weights. Given that any set of dimensions identified in the SAPS data relate to socio-structural characteristics, it is clearly possible, in principle, to construct some overall index of structural disadvantage.[2]

However, it is important to be clear at all times that the construction of such an overall index of structural disadvantage relieves neither academics nor policy makers of the task of assessing the implications of the fact that an equivalent score may result from entirely different combinations of socio-structural disadvantage arising from quite distinct socio-economic processes and requiring radically different responses.

Implications for Area-Based Interventions

In considering the implications for area-based interventions of the evidence presented here it is necessary to make clear that it is not part of our brief to offer evaluations of specific programmes. Any such evaluation would need to be designed in light of the specific objectives of the programme being assessed. Instead our objective is to ensure that the debate relating to such interventions is informed by an accurate understanding of the extent to which poverty is concentrated and the likely consequences of such concentration. In attempting to develop our own position it may be helpful if we use as reference points two arguments for area-based intervention which involve rather different justifications.

The first argument for such intervention is found in the NESC's (1994) *Report on a New Approach to Rural Development*. Here it is argued that it is possible to disentangle the idea of an area-based approach from the idea of a selective approach. Here one would simply accept, that despite earlier advocacy of such interventions on the basis of targeting and the development of an appropriate response to cumulative disadvantage, the accumulating evidence relating to the geographical distribution of unemployment and poverty suggests that all areas are affected by serious problems of this sort. In consequence one can conclude that:

> "...area-based policies can make an effective contribution to policy, and if all areas contain substantial numbers of unemployed or people in poverty, then a case can be made for the adoption of an area-based approach." (NESC, 1994: 93)

---

[2] Although the problems involved in so doing are by no means trivial.

This approach it appears would primarily consist of more effective design and delivery of programmes by national agencies.

An alternative perspective is offered by Haase et al., (1996: 9) when they consider the implications of the spatially pervasive nature of poverty for area-based interventions. They argue that:

> "While the spatially uneven outcomes of the social and economic development of Irish society are clearly the product of underlying structural change, they nevertheless take on a distinct spatial dimension in the way they manifest themselves. Furthermore, this spatial dimension is increasingly seen to have an independent effect on the degree of social exclusion experienced by those living in those areas." (Haase et al., 1996: 9)

Our current analysis confirms our earlier findings (Nolan, Whelan and Williams, 1994) that from a targeting perspective the use of variables such as unemployment or unskilled manual social class can provide only a very crude instrument in reaching the relevant "at risk" populations. Area-based strategies cannot be the panacea for spatially pervasive problems of poverty and unemployment. National economic and social policies are vital. Confronted by the evidence that poverty and unemployment are not concentrated in a limited set of areas the conclusion that the principal objective of area-based interventions should relate to improving the design and implementation of national policy seems to be a compelling one. However, our capacity to distinguish between poor and non-poor households on the basis of tenure suggests that there may still be an important case to be made for targeting-related arguments.

Fifty per cent of poor households are located in the private sector and the evidence suggests that very little possibility exists of precise targeting of such households. Furthermore, it is difficult to see how notions of cumulative disadvantage or an independent spatial dimension have any great relevance for this group. In those cases, the most plausible justification for area-based intervention aimed at reducing poverty would seem to be one which emphasises decentralisation, participation and co-ordination of national inputs. By contrast, directing resources to local authority households will be successful in reaching a relatively high number of poor households. This will be even more the case if the group targeted is public sector renters, especially in urban centres and more particularly Dublin. Overall, lack of concentration of poverty should not blind us to the fact that substantial opportunities exist for area-based interventions which offer the possibility of particularly effective forms of targeting of scarce resources.

While area-based interventions in local authority areas could be justified solely on the basis of effective targeting and co-ordination, it does seem important to distinguish between interventions solely justified on this basis and those which have the additional justification of conforming to the principle of selectivity. Apart from any argument relating to the superior claim to resources of the latter, the type of intervention appropriate would seem likely to be different in each case. The particular attraction of targeted interventions has been the possibility they have of counteracting cumulative processes of disadvantage and their consequences. However, in our efforts to devise appropriate forms of intervention in poverty "blackspots" it is important to keep in mind the fact that, while public sector housing provides us with an indicator of poverty which facilitates targeting, this does not constitute evidence that such poverty is, in any genuinely causal sense, a consequence of location in such housing. Even in the case of local authority renters, our unexplained residual effect represents the maximum effect of such factors. In further work we will take advantage of a range of information in the 1994 survey relating to households' perceptions of their areas in order to provide a more rigorous assessment of the role of area *per se*. In addition, it is necessary to stress that the creation of areas of homogenous deprivation is a consequence not simply of individual social selection but also of national housing policies. It is crucial that, having contributed to the creation of areas characterised by minimal resources, the state does not develop unrealistic expectations of the extent to which the communities which reside in them can find the solution to the problems which characterise those areas. This is particularly true where intervention is primarily at the level of individual capacity rather than community resources.

One of the strongest arguments currently for area-based interventions, in areas dominated by local authority tenants, may relate, not so much to the independent role which location in such areas plays in creating unemployment or poverty, but to the distinctive consequences of deprivation in such areas for the individuals involved and for the level of social integration in the society as a whole. The degree to which some groups are becoming increasingly fatalistic, disillusioned and detached from social and political institutions, and the extent to which any such detachment is a consequence of polarisation between different social groups or locations, are key questions which we are pursuing in our ongoing research programme. It is in developing our understanding of such processes, and the role which empowerment of local communities can play in counteracting them, that we are likely to find a justification for community development.

Appendix

Rural District Reference Map

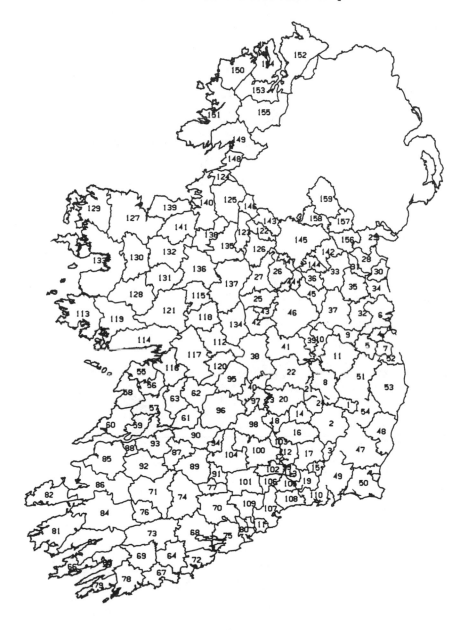

CARLOW
1 BALTINGLASS No.2
R.D.
2 CARLOW R.D. *
3 IDRONE R.D.

DUBLIN
4 DUBLIN COUNTY
BOROUGH
5 DUBLIN-BELGARD
6 DUBLIN-FINGAL
7 DUN LAOGHAIRE/
RATHDOWN

KILDARE
8 ATHY No. 1 R.D. *
9 CELBRIDGE No. 1 R.D.
10 EDENDERRY No. 2
R.D.
11 NAAS No. 1 R.D. *

KILKENNY
12 CALLAN R.D.
13 CK-ON-SUIR No. 3
R.D.
14 CASTLECOMER R.D.
15 IDA R.D.
16 KILKENNY R.D. *
17 THOMASTOWN R.D.
18 URLINGFORD R.D.
19 WATERFORD No. 2
R.D.

LAOIS
20 ABBEYLEIX R.D.
21 ATHY No. 2 R.D.
22 MOUNTMELLICK
R.D.
23 ROSCREA No. 3 R.D.
24 SLIEVEMARGY R.D.

LONGFORD
25 BALLYMAHON R.D.
26 GRANARD No. 1 R.D.
27 LONGFORD R.D. *

LOUTH
28 ARDEE No. 1 R.D.
29 DUNDALK R.D. *
30 LOUTH R.D. *

MEATH
31 ARDEE No. 2 R.D.
32 DUNSHAUGHLIN
R.D.
33 KELLS R.D. *

34 MEATH R.D.
35 NAVAN R.D. *
36 OLDCASTLE R.D.
37 TRIM R.D. *

OFFALY
38 BIRR No. 1 R.D. *
39 EDENDERRY No. 1
R.D.
40 ROSCREA No. 2 R.D.
41 TULLAMORE R.D. *

WESTMEATH
42 ATHLONE No. 1 R.D. *
43 BALLYMORE R.D.
44 COOLE R.D.
45 DELVIN R.D.
46 MULLINGAR R.D.

WEXFORD
47 ENNISCORTHY R.D. *
48 GOREY R.D.
49 NEW ROSS R.D. *
50 WEXFORD R.D. *

WICKLOW
51 BALTINGLASS No.1
R.D.
52 RATHDOWN No. 2
R.D. *
53 RATHDRUM R.D. *
54 SHILLELAGH R.D.

CLARE
55 BALLYVAGHAN R.D.
56 CORROFIN R.D.
57 ENNIS R.D. *
58 ENNISTIMON R.D.
59 KILLADYSERT R.D.
60 KILRUSH R.D. *
61 MEELICK R.D.
62 SCARRIFF R.D.
63 TULLA R.D.

CORK COUNTY
64 BANDON R.D.
65 BANTRY R.D.
66 CASTLETOWN R.D.
67 CLONAKILTY R.D. *
68 CORK R.D. *
69 DUNMANWAY R.D.
70 FERMOY R.D. *
71 KANTURK R.D.
72 KINSALE R.D. *
73 MACROOM R.D. *
74 MALLOW R.D. *

75 MIDLETON R.D. *
76 MILLSTREET R.D.
77 MITCHELSTOWN
No.1 R.D.
78 SKIBBEREEN R.D. *
79 SKULL R.D.
80 YOUGHAL No. 1 R.D. *

KERRY
81 CAHERSIVEEN R.D.
82 DINGLE R.D.
83 KENMARE R.D.
84 KILLARNEY R.D. *
85 LISTOWEL R.D. *
86 TRALEE R.D. *

LIMERICK COUNTY
87 CROOM R.D.
88 GLIN R.D.
89 KILMALLOCK R.D.
90 LIMERICK No. 1
R.D. *
91 MITCHELSTOWN
No.2 R.D.
92 NEWCASTLE R.D.
93 RATHKEALE R.D.
94 TIPPERARY No. 2 R.D.

TIPPERARY N.R.
95 BORRISOKANE R.D.
96 NENAGH R.D. *
97 ROSCREA No. 1 R.D.
98 THURLES R.D. *

TIPPERARY S.R.
99 CK-ON-SUIR No.1
R.D.*
100 CASHEL R.D. *
101 CLOGHEEN R.D.
102 CLONMEL No. 1
R.D.*
103 SLIEVARDAGH R.D.
104 TIPPERARY No. 1
R.D. *

WATERFORD COUNTY
105 CK-ON-SUIR No. 2
R.D.
106 CLONMEL No. 2 R.D.
107 DUNGARVAN R.D. *
108 KILMACTHOMAS
R.D.
109 LISMORE R.D.
110 WATERFORD No. 1
R.D. *
111 YOUGHAL No. 2 R.D.

GALWAY
112 BALLINASLOE No.1
R.D. *
113 CLIFDEN R.D.
114 GALWAY R.D. *
115 GLENNAMADDY
R.D.
116 GORT R.D.
117 LOUGHREA R.D.
118 MOUNT BELLEW
R.D.
119 OUGHTERARD R.D.
120 PORTUMNA R.D.
121 TUAM R.D.

LEITRIM
122 BALLINAMORE R.D.
123 CK-ON-SH'NON No.1
R.D
124 KINLOUGH R.D.
125 MANORHAMILTON
R.D.
126 MOHILL R.D.

MAYO
127 BALLINA R.D. *
128 BALLINROBE R.D.
129 BELMULLET R.D.
130 CASTLEBAR R.D. *
131 CLAREMORRIS R.D.
132 SWINEFORD R.D.
133 WESTPORT R.D. *

ROSCOMMON
134 ATHLONE No. 2 R.D.
135 BOYLE No. 1 R.D.
136 CASTLEREAGH R.D.
137 ROSCOMMON R.D.

SLIGO
138 BOYLE No. 2 R.D.
139 DROMORE WEST
R.D.
140 SLIGO R.D. *
141 TOBERCURRY R.D.

CAVAN
142 BAILIEBOROUGH
R.D.
143 BAWNBOY R.D.
144 CASTLERAHAN R.D.
145 CAVAN R.D. *
146 ENNISKILLEN No.2
R.D.
147 MULLAGHORAN
R.D.

DONEGAL
148 BALLYSHANNON
R.D. *
149 DONEGAL R.D.
150 DUNFANAGHY R.D.
151 GLENTIES R.D.
152 INISHOWEN R.D. *
153 LETTERKENNY
R.D. *
154 MILLFORD R.D.
155 STRANORLAR R.D.

MONAGHAN
156 CARRICK-MACROSS
R.D. *
157 CASTLEBLAYNEY
R.D. *
158 CLONES No. 1 R.D. *
159 MONAGHAN R.D. *

(Denotes that the district
contains an Urban
District; Municipal
Borough; or Co. Borough)*

Bibliography

ADM (1994): Community Development within Local Development: Proceedings of a meeting held on 29th & 30th September, 1994.

Callan, T., Nolan, B., Whelan, B.J. and Hannan, D.F. with Creighton, S. (1989): *Poverty, Income and Welfare in Ireland*, Dublin: Economic and Social Research Institute.

Callan, T., Nolan, B. and Whelan, C.T. (1993): "Resources, Deprivation and the Measurement of Poverty", *Journal of Social Policy*, 5, 3: 243–262.

Callan, T. and Nolan, B. (1994): "Poverty and Unemployment", in Nolan, B. and. Callan, T. (eds.), *Poverty and Policy in Ireland*, Dublin: Gill and Macmillan.

Callan, T., Nolan, B., Whelan, B.J., Whelan, C.T. and Williams, J. (1996): *Poverty in the 1990s: Evidence From the Living in Ireland Survey*, Dublin: Oak Tree Press.

Clark, W.A.V. and Avery, K.L. (1976): "The Effects of Data Aggregation in Statistical Analysis", *Geographical Analysis*, Vol. (viii), October.

Coyle, C. (1996): "Local and Regional Administrative Structures and Rural Poverty", in Curtin, C., Haase, T. and Tovey, H. (eds.), *Poverty in Rural Ireland*, Dublin: Oak Tree Press.

Craig, S. and McKeown, K. (1994): *Progress Through Partnership*, Dublin: Combat Poverty Agency.

Curtin, C. (1996): "Back to the Future" in Curtin, C., Haase, T. and Tovey, H. (eds.), *Poverty in Rural Ireland*, Dublin: Oak Tree Press.

Fahy, T. and Watson, D. (1995): *An Analysis of Social Housing Need*, Dublin: Economic and Social Research Institute.

FitzGerald, J. and Keegan, O. (1993): "The Community Support Framework 1989–1993: Evaluations and Recommendations for the 1994–1997 Framework", Dublin: Stationery Office.

Fotheringham, A.S. and Wong, D.W.S. (1991): "The Modifiable Areal Unit Problem in Multivariate Statistical Analysis", *Environment and Planning*, 23.

Frazer, H. (1996): "The Role of Community Development in Local Development" in *Partnership in Action — The Role of Community Development and Partnership in Ireland*, Galway: Community Workers Co-operative.

Gehlke, C.E. and Biehl, K. (1934): "Certain Effects of Grouping upon the Size of the Correlation Co-efficient in Census Tract Material", *Journal of the American Statistical Association Supplement*, Vol. 29

Haase, T., McKeown, K. and Rourke, S. (1996): *Local Development Strategies for Disadvantaged Areas, 1992–1995: Evaluation of the Global Grant in Ireland*, Dublin: Area Development Management (ADM) Ltd.

Liao, T.F. (1994): *Interpreting Probability Models: Logit, Probit and Other Generalized Linear Models,* London: Sage.

Menard, S. (1995): *Applied Logistic Regression Analysis*, London: Sage.

National Economic and Social Council (1990): *Strategies for the Nineties: Economic Stability and Structural Change*; Report No. 89, Dublin: NESC.

National Economic and Social Council (1993): *A Strategy for Competitiveness, Growth and Employment*; Report No. 96, Dublin: NESC.

National Economic and Social Council (1995): *A New Approach to Rural Development*; Report No. 97, Dublin: NESC.
Nolan, B., Whelan, C.T and Williams, J. (1994): "Spatial Aspects of Poverty and Disadvantage" in Nolan, B. and Callan, T., *Poverty and Policy*, Dublin: Gill and Macmillan.

Nolan, B. and Whelan, C.T. (1996): *Resources, Deprivation and Poverty*, Oxford: Clarendon Press.

Oppenshaw, S. and Taylor, P.J. (1982): "The Modifiable Areal Unit Problem" in Wrigley, N. and Bennett, R.J. (eds.) *Quantitative Geography: A British View*, London: Routledge and Keegan.

Oppenshaw, S. (1984a): "Ecological Fallacies and the Analysis of Areal Census Data", *Environment and Planning*, Vol. 16.

Oppenshaw, S. (1984b): "The Modifiable Areal Unit Problem" *Concepts and Techniques in Modern Geography*, No. 38, Norwich: Geo Books.

Organisation for Economic Co-operation and Development (1996): *Ireland: Local Partnerships and Social Innovation*, Paris: OECD.

Pringle, D. (1996): *Something Old, Something New . . . Lessons to be Learnt From Previous Strategies of Positive Territorial Discrimination*, Annual Conference of the Geographical Society of Ireland, Maynooth, September.

Roche, J. (1984): *Poverty and Income Maintenance Policies in Ireland*, Dublin: Institute for Public Administration.

Rottman, D.B., Hannan, D.F., Hardiman, N., and Wiley, M. (1982): *The Distribution of Income in the Republic of Ireland: A Study in Social Class and Family — Cycle Inequalities*, Dublin: Economic and Social Research Institute.

Rourke, S. (1994): *Local Development in the Republic of Ireland: An Overview and Analysis*, unpublished report for the Combat Poverty Agency.

Sen, A. (1983): "Poor, Relatively Speaking", *Oxford Economic Papers*, 37: 669–76.

Shortall, S. (1994): "The Irish Rural Development Paradigm — An Exploratory Analysis", *Economic and Social Review*, 25:3, 233–260.
Walsh, J. (1996): *Tackling Poverty Through Spatial Intervention*: Annual Conference of the Geographical Society of Ireland, Maynooth, September.

Whelan, C.T., Hannan, D.F. and Creighton, S. (1991), *Unemployment, Poverty and Psychological Distress*, Dublin: Economic and Social Research Institute.

Williams, J. (1993) *Spatial Variations in Deprivation Surrogates — A Preliminary Analysis*, unpublished report for the Combat Poverty Agency.

Yule, G.U. and Kendall, M.G. (1950): *An Introduction to the Theory of Statistics*, London: Griffen.